Hf

GAY ESCORT AND CLIENT
TO BEST FRIENDS FOR LIFE

A TRUE STORY

by

ALEXANDER BRILEE

Alexander Brilee

Contents

Contents	3
Preface	5
Prologue	6
Lee's Early Years	7
Lee at Sagging Elm	13
Lee at Mansea Hall	20
Lee's Life After Leaving Mansea Hall	28
Lee at 16	33
Brian's Early Years	38
Brian's Early Professional Career	48
Brian's First Visit To London	55
Brian As a Professor	61
Rachel	67
Brian and Lee's First Meeting	69
Their First Trip	73
Back in London	76
Lee in College	80
Chrissy and Tiger	82
Lee in California	84
Their First House	88
Brian and Lee's Relationship	93
Brian and Lee's Travels	99
Brian's Vertigo	104
Brian's Prostate Cancer	110
Lee's Maternal Grandmother	117
Religion	125
Opera	129

Jewish Food   **134**

Brian Aging   **136**

Virus   **144**

Epilogue   **151**

Preface

This is a true story. Names and some details have been changed to protect privacy. A dual memoir is an unusual format, but it is completely appropriate for this book. It was written together by two people, Brian and Lee. Some of it is about Lee's life, some of it is about Brian's life, but most of it is about their long friendship. Why is only one author shown if two people wrote this memoir? There are indeed two authors. We chose for simplicity to use only one pseudonym to represent both authors. The grammar and spelling will be American throughout, but some of the terminology will be British when the people and places described are British.

Prologue

The advice that you'll find on the web for someone thinking about calling an escort is that you should never call an escort if you're looking for a friend. During the first 68 years of Brian's life he could not argue with that advice. He had picked up hitchhikers on the street, responded to ads in a gay newspaper and visited gay brothels in several countries. While he had some satisfying sexual encounters, and even saw a few escorts for more than a year each, he had never met anyone in that way whom he could regard as a true friend. And how could he believe that someone he had met in that way was really a friend?

The common advice to prospective escorts parallels the advice to prospective clients. An escort should not think of a client as a friend. Is it possible then to go from an escort-client relationship to a relationship of best friends and for that new relationship to last? Yes, it is. For Brian and Lee this friendship has lasted for more than 17 years and continues to this day. Skeptics might protest that Brian cares only about receiving sexual gratification from Lee and that Lee cares only about receiving financial assistance from Brian, but they both know that their friendship is genuine. Before looking at how this friendship began, let's consider what Lee's life was like before he met Brian and what Brian's life was like before he met Lee.

Lee's Early Years

Lee was born in 1986. He had a difficult childhood and the difficulties continued into his late teens. His first memory was being trapped in a dark tunnel and hearing a loud up-and-down screaming sound. It was terrifying. He didn't know what it was but he felt that it was something really bad. He learned later from his mum that when he was six months old she was pushing him in a pram on Lambeth Bridge. What seemed like a dark tunnel to Lee as an infant was the large hood of the pram. An ambulance passed by with its siren wailing. Lee screamed and started to cry. His mum said that she had never before seen him cry like that.

Lee also remembers that his mum would sometimes leave him in his pram while she chatted with her friends. It was as if he wasn't even there. He tried to open the clip to get out of the pram, but it was too difficult for him to do it with his fingers. He finally learned to open the clip with his teeth. When he got out they grabbed him and put him back in the pram.

As soon as Lee was able to walk he became very adventurous. He liked to climb everywhere. He climbed onto the wardrobe. He created games in which he would climb around the house without touching the floor. Lee doesn't have any memories of his mum or dad talking to him when he was very young. He believes that they probably never did. He enjoyed staying with his nan and his granddad because they would talk to him, but never in a childish way. They would talk to him as if he were an adult.

Lee's mum suffered from postnatal depression and was in and out of mental hospitals until Lee was around two. His nan mothered him in his early years. Lee enjoyed talking with his granddad, but when Lee was four his granddad was riddled with cancer. Lee remembers feeding him chocolate éclairs because his granddad couldn't feed himself. He also remembers lighting his granddad's pipe and the flame coming back out and burning his thumb.

When Lee was a small child his mum was young, just in her twenties. Lee thought that she was beautiful. She was slim and looked very tall to him. Her long black hair was straight and shiny. It went just past her shoulders and she had a fringe. Lee remembers one time visiting his mum's friend and her calling him a Damien child because he threw tantrums. He would mimic what his mum and her friend were saying to wind them up. His mum's friend would say, "You're a little Damien, you are," and he would imitate her, "You're a little Damien, you are." She would respond to his imitation with, "Isn't that scary," and he would just imitate that as well, "Isn't that scary." His mum's friend couldn't put up with his imitating behavior. She told his mum that she'd have to leave.

When they got back home, Lee was playing with some colorful wooden toy bricks. He threw a bunch of them in the air and one of them accidently hit his mum on the head. He really wasn't aiming it at her head. She grabbed the metal pipe from the vacuum cleaner and hit his arm hard. He was crying for hours. But after she did it she couldn't believe what she had done and she cried and said that she was sorry. Lee was two or three at the time. After that he didn't trust his mum that much. He would no longer go to her for comfort. Instead, he would go to his dad.

Lee's dad was slim and not bad looking. He had dark skin, dark hair and dark eyes and looked strong and scary. He was from Turkey, but other children would call him a "Paki," a derogatory term for a Pakistani. Unfortunately his parents did not take care of themselves as they grew older. His mum gained weight from drinking and his dad lost all of his teeth.

Even as a toddler, Lee witnessed arguments between his dad and his mum. His dad's shouting was so loud that the neighbors from the floor below would bang on their ceiling and the neighbors from the floor above would bang on their floor. His mum was afraid of his dad. Once he hit her over the head with a large catalog, knocking her to the ground.

One day Lee was sitting on his dad's lap and playing about with his dad's top and pulling it. His dad told him to stop, but he continued laughing and joking and playing with his top. The next thing he remembers was his dad's hand whacking him hard on his face. He never went to his dad for comfort again.

Lee remembers numerous traumatizing instances of physical abuse from his dad. When he was 5 or 6 he was making noise on a window ledge and his dad pulled him off and threw him to the floor so hard that some of his teeth were knocked out. He saw teeth on the floor and his whole mouth was bleeding.

The physical abuse by his dad continued throughout Lee's childhood. He suffered punches, suffocation and objects being thrown at him. Once his dad threw a cup at him so hard that his hip was injured and he couldn't walk for some time. Another time his dad threw a metal hamster cage at Lee's head. Lee still has a scar from this on the top of his head. Another time his dad punched him in the back so hard that he passed out and his mum thought that his dad had killed him. More than once his dad jumped on top of him and suffocated him with a duvet and only took it off when he passed out and stopped moving. After that happened a few times Lee pretended to pass out sooner so that his dad would get off him. Lee would try to get away from his terrible home life by visiting his nan. She lived a few miles away and he walked to her flat whenever he could.

Lee does have some positive memories of his dad. His dad knew that he liked Tina Turner. Lee first heard her singing on the radio. When he was five his dad recorded her concert, "Live From Barcelona 1990" on VHS. Lee really enjoyed the recording and played it over and over until the tape was worn out. Lee felt the love that Tina was expressing to her audience, a love that he had lacked at his home. When he watched the energy and joy with which she performed, it took him to a different place, away from the abuse and depression in his unhappy home.

Another positive memory that Lee has about his dad is that his dad once took him to the agency where he worked as a cleaner when he went there to pick up his paycheck. Then he took him to a store and bought a Walkman and a tape of Tina Turner's "Break Every Rule." This was something that Lee really appreciated.

The only person to whom Lee could speak and whom he could trust as a child was his nan. She gave him a fair share of beatings with mops and brooms but only if he really did something wrong, not for innocently playing.

Lee started primary school when he was five years old. He remembers his first day. He got up early. It was the beginning of winter. It was gray outside and the moon was still visible. That seemed strange to him. He didn't remember seeing the moon in the daytime before. His mum's flat was on the second floor and he was staring out the window at the cars driving by on a busy road with their headlights on. He wanted this part of the day to last longer.

He dreaded going to a place with a lot of strangers.

His mother never had much money, so he never had decent clothes or a good haircut. She cut his hair with shears and she didn't do a very good job of it. The other kids called him "mop head." He had terrible clothes, a worn knitted jumper and shoes that were too small and breaking. He felt that he looked like a tramp. The kids at school used to take the piss out of him all the time and he didn't have any friends there.

His experiences with the teacher were negative from his very first day. She told the children to sit with their legs crossed. All of the other children had been to nursery school where they had learned the expected way to do this. Lee had not been to nursery school and had not been taught at home what was meant by sitting with one's legs crossed. He didn't know what he was supposed to do and he just sat with his back against the wall. The teacher asked why he was not sitting with his legs crossed and he replied that he didn't know how to do that. The other children, who had been taught previously how they were supposed to sit, laughed at him. This made Lee want to leave school. The teacher thought he was just being stubborn and sent him to the head teacher's office.

Lee remembers going past the receptionist's desk and entering the head teacher's office. The head teacher sat in a Chesterfield swivel chair behind a mahogany desk. She had several potted plants next to her window. She told Lee that he was to stand bent over and holding his ankles for 30 minutes as punishment. Standing in that position was painful from the start. It hurt so much that he started to cry after only 10 minutes. He could see his tears dripping onto the dark red carpet in her office. Each drop darkened the carpet more where it landed. He remembers this well because it was all that he could see. He was too scared to look up and see where she was in the room.

Fifteen minutes later the pain became even more unbearable. His hands rose slowly up to his knees. The head teacher pulled a stick out of one of her potted plants and struck his legs with it. She shouted, "I told you to hold your ankles."

It was a light blow and he took it as a warning. Then she slammed the stick hard on her desk to emphasize the warning. Lee continued to hold his ankles. Two other children were in the head teacher's office undergoing the same punishment and the three children were crying together. Finally, the half hour was up and she let him go. The head teacher was clearly breaking the law. Forcing someone to hold an uncomfortable position, let alone a painful position, is corporal punishment and had been outlawed in English schools.

In another incident at his primary school, a substitute teacher told the children to draw rain in their notebooks. Lee drew a series of vertical lines to represent rain. Later the head teacher looked in his book and saw that drawing. She yelled at Lee for scribbling in his notebook and again made him hold his ankles as punishment.

Lee had other problems with his primary school teacher. He had difficulty writing and his teacher would come over to him and criticize his work. The other children could hear her doing this and they would laugh at him. He felt humiliated and he began to skip school by sliding back under the gate after his dad dropped him off. One day when he returned home he told his dad that he didn't want to go to school because of the way the teacher and the other children treated him. His dad just made it worse. He went into the school with Lee and started shouting in Lee's classroom in front of the other children. This was so embarrassing that Lee didn't want to go to that school anymore.

Lee had great difficulty with spelling. When the teacher asked him to spell a simple word and he couldn't do it, the other children laughed and put up their hands indicating that they could spell the word. The teacher accused Lee of not having been paying attention when she had gone over the spelling of the word in a previous lesson.

The teacher and the other kids made Lee feel dumb, even in primary school, but he was really very clever and he outsmarted the other kids. He took a piece of paper and drew a vertical line down the middle. He walked around the schoolyard imitating the mannerisms of a teacher and told the kids that he was making a list of who was good and who was bad. To make this seem real he started by going up to kids who had been nice to him and telling them that they would be on the good list. He pretended to write their names on the piece of paper. They were pleased and the other kids could see that. Then he went up to kids who had been mean to him, ridiculing him when he had difficulty reading or spelling. He told them that he was putting them on the bad list and he pretended to write their names on his paper. The kids really believed him and some of those he told he was putting on the bad list started to cry.

Lee didn't understand why spelling was so difficult for him and this caused him to act up at school. One time when his teacher asked him to spell some words and he wasn't able to, the teacher accused him of being lazy and not trying. He got very frustrated and knocked over his desk. The teacher said, "That's it!" and she grabbed him by the arm and started to drag him to the head teacher's office. They had to go outside to get there. It was raining and the ground was slippery. There were three small steps with a banister on the way.

Lee didn't want to go to the head teacher's office where he knew he would be subjected to the painful punishment of holding his ankles for a long period of time. He was trying to hold onto the banister and his teacher was trying to pull him down the steps. She slipped and fell on her backside. When they arrived at the head teacher's office, his teacher was disheveled from her fall and the head teacher asked what had happened. Lee's teacher lied, saying that Lee had pushed her down the stairs. Lee was expelled from his primary school at the age of seven.

Lee at Sagging Elm

It was not until Lee was an adult that he learned that he was dyslexic. It was because of dyslexia that he had great difficulty reading aloud in class and completing writing assignments. As a result of this he did very little work at school. Dyslexia was well known at the time and it should have been obvious to his teachers that he was dyslexic, but no one on the staff at his primary school or later at his secondary school made the effort to have him tested. A timely diagnosis of his dyslexia might have made a big difference in Lee's early life.

Lee's mum tried to find a school for him after he was expelled from his primary school, but no school wanted to admit a boy who had a record of pushing his teacher down stairs, although he had not actually done that. His mum kept trying. Lee was out of school for three years and was finally offered a place in a school called Sagging Elm.

Sagging Elm was no ordinary school. It was a school for children with behavioral problems. There were children at that school who had been charged with robbery, assault and other serious offenses. Lee had never done anything like that and he felt uncomfortable being placed in such a school. The kids at the school were smoking and talking about stealing and about being in trouble with the police. They constantly bullied Lee. A 13-year-old boy named Paul started to hang out with Lee. Paul was tough and the other boys were afraid of him. He protected Lee from the bullies. But there was a price to pay. He had to go out stealing every day with Paul. He didn't like doing it, but he had to do it so that he wouldn't be bullied at school. Paul wore a puffer jacket so that he could hide items that he stole from shops.

Things got much worse with Paul. He had been grooming Lee for something else. One day Paul asked Lee to come with him to a friend's flat. He said it was "well good" at his friend's flat and that his friend had an electric train set. Lee used to love trains so it sounded fun. When he got to his friend's flat it turned out that the "friend" was a man in his forties. Indeed the man's bedroom was completely covered in little railway tracks. As Lee started to play with the electric train set, his so-called friend Paul came up behind him with a knife. He grabbed Lee and held the knife to his neck. Then he took him into the other room where the older guy was waiting.

Paul took Lee to the older man's flat day after day for nearly a year. He was getting money for bringing Lee there. He said to Lee, "If you say anything about this I'll tell everybody at school what you did."

At the time this would have been very embarrassing for Lee. He definitely didn't want his mother or father to find out anything about this so he just carried on going round there.

There were other problems with Paul. He was with Lee at a tube station and for no apparent reason he took out a knife and stabbed Lee in the leg. Lee didn't realize what had happened at first until he felt blood running down his leg. It felt warm at first and then felt cooler. The staff at the station called an ambulance and Lee was taken to a hospital where they disinfected and dressed the wound.

It appeared that Paul was starting to blackmail the older man. Lee overheard a phone conversation between them. "I need £40, not twenty," Paul said.

"I haven't got £40; I only got twenty," the older man said.

"If you don't give me £40 I'm going to tell everyone what you did."

Lee could hear that the older man was panicking. That's all that Lee could remember about what was said. After arguing with the older man, Paul must have told the other kids at school what the man had been doing to Lee. One morning when Lee arrived at school a group of kids was standing around outside. When they saw Lee they started saying things like, "Get away from me chi chi man. How could you do that, taking it up the ass? You nasty little batty boy."

They said a lot of other stuff too. Lee was overwhelmed with embarrassment, shame and anger. He picked up a fire extinguisher and used it to smash four or five windows. When the head teacher approached him he sprayed him with the fire extinguisher. He was expelled and that's what he wanted to happen. He didn't want to go to that school anymore

After smashing the windows, Lee ran away as far as he could, which was only to Brixton. He stayed out all night. The police found him the next day and took him home. He believed that his mother had found out what had been happening to him. He was so embarrassed that he couldn't even look at her. The police came round the next day and a policewoman sat down next to Lee. She said, "You have to come to the station."

He really didn't want to go but he went anyway. When he got there the police asked him all sorts of questions about the child molester. They said, "Did he touch you inappropriately? Did he come on to you in any way? Please try and remember, Lee, anything at all," the policewoman said in a nice voice.

She assured him that he wasn't in any trouble. He knew that she must have known that something had happened. He knew that what the man did to him was considered disgusting and he was afraid that he would be considered disgusting if he told anyone about it. He was so embarrassed that he couldn't speak. He didn't even say one word. He saw a lot of cameras in the room and he knew that he was being recorded. He was so stressed that he just wanted to get out of there. He doesn't remember if anything happened to the man who molested him. All he remembers was feeling glad that it was over and that he didn't have to see Paul anymore and that the abuse would stop.

When Lee was around nine he liked to visit Brixton station, the southern terminus of the Victoria Line. The arriving train drivers would walk along the platform from the southern end of the train to the northern end to enter the cab for the return trip. Lee would approach a driver and ask him something about what it was like to drive a train. Some of the drivers would let him ride in the cab and one driver even let him control the train for a while. He did not stop it fast enough at one station and the train overshot the platform. The driver had to announce that passengers would not be able to exit from the first set of doors in the front carriage.

Around that time Lee saw a documentary about the new Eurostar service between London, Paris and Brussels. The sleek shiny trains that were brand new at the time fascinated him. He would go to Brixton station which was near his home to watch the Eurostar trains pass by. He sometimes went there with his mum, telling her that some day he would take her to Paris on Eurostar. He did this as an adult many years later. One day he found a way to get onto the Eurostar platform at Waterloo undetected. He was around 10 at the time. He boarded the train and probably could have gone all the way to Paris, but he decided to get off before the train started to move.

Lee has three younger brothers and a younger sister. Adrian is two years younger, Mark is four years younger, Christopher is six years younger and Sarah is eight years younger. They lived with their mum and dad in a tiny two-bedroom flat in South London. Lee's mum would say, "We'll be moving soon," to which Lee replied, "Whatever, you always say that."

A few months later they did move into a four-bedroom house. Lee remembers when he first saw the house. He thought it was really wonderful, with green grass in the garden and lovely white walls. He would finally have his own room instead of sharing with his brothers. His mother looked happy. He was pleased to see her happy for a change, but her happiness didn't last long.

Lee noticed a large number of caravans next to his mum's new house. It was the "travelers." A woman from one of the caravans offered his mum a cup of tea, which she accepted. Lee thought to himself that this was big mistake. Accepting a cup of tea from that woman was the worst thing his mum could have done. From then on the people from the caravans were asking for things all the time. They never paid for anything. One woman told Lee's mum that the milkman would not deliver to the caravans and asked her to buy a bottle of milk for her. Lee's mum was a kind but naive person and it seemed like a reasonable request. But soon it was two bottles, then four bottles and then a whole case. It was the camel with a cold nose.

Another woman from the caravans asked Lee's mum to order a lawn mower from her catalog and Lee's mum ordered it on her own account. Lee knew that they wouldn't give her the money for it, but his mum wouldn't listen to him. The people who asked for it didn't have a lawn and Lee suspected that they would be selling the lawnmower that they got from his mum.

Lee's mum was afraid of the travelers and kept buying what they asked for. Her own five children went hungry sometimes because she didn't have enough money left to buy food after making the purchases for the travelers. Lee was frustrated by his mum's inability to stand up to those people, but he was only ten at the time and there wasn't much that he could do.

People from the caravans would throw trash, including used

diapers, into his mum's garden. One of their children had a catapult toy and broke the windows in Lee's house. The council repaired them but soon the windows were smashed again. Lee's mum found the sound of the windows being smashed to be quite frightening. After the windows were broken repeatedly she just left them boarded up, leaving Lee's family in a dark house with a garden filled with trash. This went on for many years.

During that time, Lee's brother Adrian made friends with four kids living in the next street who were about the same age. One of these kids, Alice, became Lee's best friend, or at least his best "partner in crime." They used to go out to the big shopping center in Croydon and steal things. They also went to Mitcham Town Centre. At the time Lee thought his excursions with Alice were fun. It turned out that Alice was not stealing for fun. She was stealing out of desperation. Her mum had died and her dad was a drug addict. She and her two brothers and her sister had no food. Social Services eventually put all four of them into care, but they placed each of them into different foster homes. This was a portent of a sad part of Lee's future when Lee and his brothers and sister would be separated and placed in different foster homes. Lee and Alice lost contact for a while after she was put into care, but they got together again a few years later.

One day before Alice was put into care she went with Lee to the park just down the bottom of the hill next to Lee's house. They met a big tall girl named Beatrice, who was playing tennis with her sister Joann at the courts in the park. Lee found Joann to be very sweet and friendly, but he thought that Beatrice was something of a bully. She started on Lee for no reason. She poked him in the eye. He went to tell her mum, Shirley. Shirley lived in the same close, just a few doors down. She seemed to be very friendly. She invited Lee into her house a few days after the incident with Beatrice. They sat and chatted for hours. He told her what had happened with Beatrice. Shirley didn't really say much about it, but she said that she would sort it out. She said, "Don't worry love, I'll have a word with her."

Lee had met Shirley briefly before, a little wave and that. She did have a word with Beatrice, but it couldn't have been very successful because Beatrice still looked as though she didn't like Lee, but he didn't care because he got to like Shirley a lot. He used to think of her as a second mum.

Shirley invited Lee to her house every day. He enjoyed going there. It was a way that he could get away from his dad's shouting. His dad really used to get on his nerves. He would hit his kids a lot for no reason and not just any little hit. He punched his sons as if they were grown men. So when Shirley invited Lee into her house, that was a way for him to escape his other life at home.

For some reason, Beatrice was jealous of the relationship between Lee and her mum. After a while Beatrice got used to the fact that Lee was just a good friend of the family. Lee started to get on with her really well and they used to go out shopping together. He would help her choose what she wanted to wear. They used to have a lot of fun. Lee enjoyed those days.

Beatrice always looked nice. She made an effort with everything and she had a smashing personality. She was also quite a tough lady. Lee remembered that no one would dare mess with Shirley's family. No, it wasn't very nice to get on the bad side of them. That was something else Lee liked about them. He always wanted to feel safe and he definitely did feel safe when he was with them.

Lee used to see Shirley as a "Mother Teresa," always helping people. She would say to him, "If you are ever hungry or there's anything that you need, anything at all, you just knock on that door and if I've got it you can have it." And that was very true. Sometimes during the night Lee would need to use asthma pumps, but would realize that his were empty. He would run from his house all wheezy, pick up little pebbles outside Shirley's house and throw them at her window. This was so he wouldn't wake anyone else during the night. Shirley would come to the window.

"Yes, love, what is it," she would say.

"Please, can I use your asthma pumps?" he replied.

She would come down the stairs half awake and give him the asthma pumps and then offer him a cup of tea. They would sit and chat about life for hours. That was one of many things that he liked about Shirley. She was always there for him. He remembers the times when Shirley would make him cry with laughter. One evening her partner Arnold returned from his construction job and took his boots off in the living room. "Lee," Shirley said, "What's that nasty smell?"

Then she ran into the bathroom, grabbed a can of air freshener and sprayed it all over her partner's feet saying, "Get out of there now and get in the bath, you dirty fat bastard!"

Her partner didn't mind. He found it amusing. She would come out with all kinds of stuff. That was just the way that Shirley was. No one could ever change her and everyone liked her that way.

Back home, Lee's mum and dad were still having problems with the travelers, not that they didn't bring a lot of it on themselves. Ever since they moved into their new house, his dad repeatedly embarrassed the family with his shouting. Lee's mum would also scream a lot, but that was because of his dad. The neighbors imitated their screaming and Lee hated that. So basically, his dad was the main cause of Lee's problems at home and he just couldn't wait to get away from it all.

Lee had problems with the travelers' teenage kids throughout most of his childhood. They would shout at him and slap his face for no reason. Once when he was walking up the hill near his home one of them hit him over the head with a full milk bottle. He passed out and doesn't remember what happened afterwards. A neighbor told him that they were kicking him while he was lying on the ground. He was able to get up and make it to his street door with his head hurting. He thought later that this attack could have been part of a gang initiation. Another time one of them pulled a gun and told him that if he didn't start running he would shoot him. Lee didn't know if the person threatening him was serious and he started running. Both of these things happened when he was 11 years old.

Lee at Mansea Hall

When Lee was 12 he was offered a place at a boarding school that specialized in teaching children with behavioral problems. It was located in the South Downs, which is designated as an area of outstanding natural beauty. Lee remembers the train journey with his mum from Waterloo. He enjoyed seeing the beautiful countryside passing by his window. At Basingstoke station Lee and his mum were greeted by a man named Dennis who drove them to the school. It seemed pretty far from the station and the area around the school seemed deserted. A large Georgian building sat at the top of a long drive. It was a grand building with a huge door and old carved wood panels on the walls.

Mr. Saxon, the head teacher, greeted them as they entered. Lee thought that he seemed really nice. Seconds later as Lee turned around he witnessed a boy throwing a big bowl of trifle up the wall and running after another boy. Lee tried so hard not to laugh. Mr. Saxon seemed very embarrassed by what had happened, but he just carried on and invited Lee and his mum into his office. Lee could see from the look on Mr. Saxon's face that he was thinking he would deal with those two boys later.

One of the things that Lee liked about Mr. Saxon that day was that he didn't pretend that the school was perfect and that the children at the school were all little angels. He said to Lee, "There'll be a lot of things that you won't like and things that you will like. So be very honest and make up your mind, because if you're having second thoughts on coming here, then don't come. But if you want to make a go of this place then we will all help you to do the best you can."

Lee couldn't wait to start. He liked the school and everything about it as soon as he got there and he adjusted well to his new school. He had been having frequent asthma attacks at his parents' home in London from early childhood. He believed that this condition was aggravated by the pollution in the city and by his mum's use of a vacuum cleaner that lacked adequate filtering. His asthma condition was greatly improved in the countryside location of Mansea Hall and it was important for him to remain at that school for this reason alone.

Almost all of the children at the school went home each weekend, but Lee did not care that much for being at home. He liked being at the school even when it was mostly empty. On one long weekend his friend Shirley visited and brought him some cigarettes. Paul had started Lee on smoking when he was 9. Lee was now addicted to smoking and worried about running out of cigarettes between trips home. On one occasion in Year 8 he discussed this with his child protection officer, Adam. Adam was a smoker himself and was sympathetic, but Lee was under age for smoking so Adam couldn't offer him any cigarettes. Adam came by Lee's room later and told Lee that he had misplaced a packet of cigarettes. He said that it probably fell out of his pocket and was on the floor somewhere. After Adam left, Lee looked along the floor and found the cigarettes. Adam asked Lee later if he had found them and Lee said no. Of course they both knew the truth.

When did Lee know that he was gay? He remembers having a crush on a male teacher in primary school. He was attracted to big muscular men. He was not interested in women and didn't like men who were effeminate. For boys at that time the word "gay" referred to something dirty and Lee understood that being gay was something that should be hidden.

A prospective teacher was interviewed while Lee was at Mansea Hall. Lee thought that the prospective teacher's behavior was effeminate. The prospective teacher was not hired. Lee asked Mr. Saxon if the prospective teacher was not hired because he was gay. Mr. Saxon said that was not the reason. Lee asked Mr. Saxon whether he would hire a male teacher who was gay. Mr. Saxon said that it would not be appropriate for a male teacher who was gay to teach at a boys school. Lee asked why then was it okay to have female teachers at the school. Mr. Saxon said that was not the same thing. Lee understood that the head teacher thought that all gay men were perverts. It was disturbing to Lee that an educated man at the beginning of the 21st century would have that attitude. Knowing that his head teacher had that attitude was damaging to Lee's self esteem.

In a conversation with Lee during Year 10, Mr. Saxon happened to mention that some of the Year 6 and 7 students were not attending class regularly. Lee proposed an incentive scheme for rewarding students who behaved well and attended class. The students would be assigned chores, such as vacuuming and assisting the maintenance staff in other ways, and would be paid for completing those chores. If a student did not attend class he was not allowed to participate in this reward scheme. Mr. Saxon liked the proposal and put Lee in charge of it. The students were eager to participate. They liked having some extra pocket money. They looked up to Lee and they liked having Lee's approval when they behaved and attended class. It was reminiscent of the pretend reward system that Lee introduced at his primary school, but this time the rewards were real. Lee's reward scheme improved class attendance and improved the behavior of the younger students. Most of the staff appreciated what Lee had accomplished with his reward scheme, but some staff members resented his influence with the staff and students. In particular they resented his having a full set of keys just as the staff members had. Some staff members, possibly including Mr. Saxon himself, wanted to take over running Lee's incentive scheme and this may have contributed to his being expelled later that year.

Unfortunately Lee's sincere efforts to get an education at Mansea Hall were doomed from the start. The school claimed that it was educating children with behavioral problems, but it was doing no such thing. It was organized only for profit. The school experience seemed pleasant to the younger students at first. They could take part in some enjoyable activities and they didn't spend much time in class. Under the surface, however, the school had a practice that was seriously damaging to students with learning disabilities. They would admit students with learning disabilities and keep them in the school in Years 6 through 9, while the government paid them a large annual sum for educating those students. They did not properly diagnose the students' learning disabilities and in that way they saved the expense of providing the assistance to which those students were entitled.

Students in England were required to take the GCSE exams in Year 11. Their performance on these exams affected their future education and employment opportunities. In Year 10, before the students took the GCSEs, Mansea Hall would find an excuse to expel each of the students with learning disabilities. The school's advertising and their reports to the government emphasized their students' success on the GCSEs and their statistics were good because only those students who could do well on the exams were allowed to remain at the school.

Of course it would not look good if they admitted that they were expelling students because the students could not do well on exams. That would be admitting that the school had failed to provide an adequate education for those students. Instead they used a devious method for expelling those students. They would find fault with the student's behavior, either at the school or at his foster home. The school knew that they could do this because it was well known that people with untreated dyslexia are likely to have behavioral problems. The governors of the school could simply wait like vultures until these problems showed up for a student and gave them an excuse for expelling that student. All of the boys at the school did not have learning difficulties. Some had other behavioral problems. Those students could obtain acceptable scores on exams and they were kept at the school, regardless of their bad behavior. Even assaulting a teacher would not get a student expelled if he was likely to do well on exams.

It is unconscionable in the 21st century for a school of any kind, let alone a school that claimed to educate children with behavioral problems, not to have provided the help that students with dyslexia needed. A student who has great difficulty with spelling should be tested for dyslexia immediately and provided with the necessary help if this difficulty is diagnosed. The necessary help includes providing the student with a device for recording classes, a computer program that transcribes voice to text, more time to take exams and one-on-one assistance in the classroom. But Mansea Hall did not test the students for dyslexia. The school may have known that they should be doing this, but they probably did not want to spend the money for the assistance that the students would need.

Lee was never tested for dyslexia as a child. He was not allowed to record classes. He was able to do his class work only when the assistant sat with him and helped him. What he needed was an assistant sitting with him for the entire time when he was working on a writing assignment, but there was only one assistant for the seven students in a class. Several of these students likely were dyslexic also and needed the assistant's continuous help, but this of course was not possible with only one assistant in the classroom.

Instead of helping Lee, some of the teachers and assistants called him lazy and would say things such as:

"You need to try, Lee."

"I can't help you alone. You have to try to write on your own."

"You were able to spell that word yesterday. Why can't you spell it now?"

"Just sound out the word and you'll be able to spell it."

The last bit of questionable advice doesn't even work for English-speaking people who are not dyslexic. Consider the person who hears the name "Gloucester" and tries to spell it.

Lee was trying very hard, but was unable to complete his class work without more assistance. It is the sort of attitude that he experienced with uninformed teachers and uncaring school administrators that causes students with dyslexia to act up in class. It makes the student think that his lack of academic success is his fault and this damages his self-esteem. Lee was made to believe that he was lazy and unwilling to do his schoolwork, but none of that was true. It was only years later that Lee learned that his difficulty in school was not his fault at all, but was the fault of the teachers and administrators who did not provide him with the assistance to which he was entitled.

Lee liked his art classes because in these classes he had an opportunity to be creative and he didn't have to do any writing. Because he was not getting the assistance that he needed, he would skip English and math classes. The school administration could see that he would not do well on the GCSEs and they looked for an excuse to expel him in Year 10.

While at Mansea Hall, Lee had been placed in several different foster homes. He was not happy with these placements, mostly because they were far from London and he wasn't able to see friends and family on weekends. He didn't stay long at each home. Even if he behaved well at a foster home, his record with Social Services of past accusations of bad behavior always followed him and the new foster parents did not want him to stay.

Lee stayed at home for a while when he was 13, but it didn't go well. His mum was afraid of the travelers and she moved in with his nan, bringing Mark, Christopher and Sarah with her. Lee and Adrian stayed at their house with their dad. Their mum was giving their dad a portion of her benefit money to buy food for Lee and

Adrian, but he spent it all on cigarettes for himself and his two sons went hungry. Adrian found some custard that his dad was saving for Christmas. He was hungry and he ate it all. When his dad found out he beat Adrian so badly that Lee and Adrian decided to go to the police. The police saw Adrian's torn clothes and the marks on his body and put Lee and Adrian under police protection. Lee hoped that he and his brother would be put in foster care and would get some food and clothes and then could return home, but that's not what happened. Social Services removed Lee and his three brothers and his sister from their parent's home and put all five of them in care at different foster homes. Lee's mum was quite upset about losing custody of her children. She started drinking and blamed Lee for taking his brother to the police.

Social Services found a foster placement for Lee near Mansea Hall. He attended a meeting with Mr. Saxon and the woman who ran the foster home. Mr. Saxon told Lee, in the presence of that woman, that his frequent changes in foster placement were detrimental to his education and that if he didn't settle into this new home he would be expelled from Mansea Hall. In retrospect Lee understands that this was just an excuse to expel him before he took the GCSEs because the school knew that he could not do well on those exams. They wanted to make it look like being expelled was his fault rather than the fault of the school for not providing the assistance that is required for a student with dyslexia. Other boys, including a friend of Lee at the school, had similar problems with spelling. It is likely that they also were dyslexic and they also were expelled.

Lee really tried to behave well in his new foster placement. He knew that he would be expelled from Mansea Hall if that carer told Mr. Saxon that he was misbehaving and he desperately wanted to stay at Mansea Hall. But the deck was already stacked against him. Lee's heartfelt efforts to fit in at this home were in vain because the carer was determined to have him expelled from Mansea Hall and was prepared to lie about his behavior. All that she was interested in was the money that she was getting for caring for, or pretending to care for, her foster children. She was getting a large amount of extra money for Lee because his record indicated that he had behavioral problems and Social Services was having difficulty placing him. Lee was staying at Mansea Hall most of the time and only stayed at the foster home on some weekends and holidays and when Mansea Hall was closed for breaks. The carer knew that she would get much more money if Lee was expelled from Mansea Hall and stayed at her home full time.

One of the other children staying at this home was a disabled girl who was badly neglected by the carer. This bothered Lee and he tried to be friendly with the girl, but the carer objected to Lee talking with her. The carer apparently was concerned that Lee would learn too much about how the girl was being treated at that foster home.

Two 16-year-old boys also were staying at that home. The carer let them do whatever they wanted. They would smoke and do drugs and she didn't care as long as she got her money. They had a pet budgie (parakeet). Lee came home one day and found the sliding door to their bedroom open. The cage was also open and the bird was gone. The carer told the boys that Lee had let it escape. Lee knew that it was the carer who had let the bird escape so that she could blame him and get him in trouble with the other boys.

Lee's memory of his stay at her home is that she made life hell for him. Ultimately she phoned Mr. Saxon and told him lies about Lee. She told him that Lee had deliberately let the other boys' pet budgie escape, that he would not listen to her and kept going out without permission, that he smoked in his room and that he used abusive language toward her. Lee overheard her conversation and tried to phone Mr. Saxon to tell his side, but Mr. Saxon would not take his calls. Instead he sent a letter to Lee telling him that he was expelled. Mr. Saxon did not try to help Lee because it was also his objective to have Lee expelled before taking the GCSEs. Lee doesn't think that was Mr. Saxon's idea. He believes that the school's governors pressured Mr. Saxon.

Lee had made many friends during his three years at Mansea Hall and he wasn't even allowed to say goodbye to them. He had been looking forward for several years to a class trip that was scheduled for the end of Year 10. He was expecting to travel to Paris in a group with Mr. Saxon. Mr. Saxon was into French cooking and had promised to show the students some nice local restaurants. Lee had never been abroad and this trip was very important to him. He was expelled before the end of Year 10, however, and he never got to go on the trip. Lee had suffered direct abuse as a small child. His expulsion from the school that he loved because of uncaring and greedy adults was a more insidious form of abuse. Lee had never had a stable home life. Mansea Hall had been his anchor and now he was set adrift in an ocean of users.

After being expelled from Mansea Hall, Lee was expected to stay at the same foster home on a full time basis as his deceitful foster carer had intended. This was more than Lee could bear and he cut his wrists. He didn't really want to die, but he was desperate to get out of that horrible foster home. He was taken to a hospital by ambulance where he was interviewed by a psychiatrist. Lee told the psychiatrist that if he were forced to return to the same foster home he would cut his throat. The psychiatrist didn't think he would really do that, but he could see Lee's desperation and he arranged for Lee to be placed in a different foster home. Lee still had to attend a meeting with Social Services that included the woman who had been his foster carer. Knowing that she was losing the income that she had plotted to secure by keeping Lee at her home, she became verbally abusive and demonstrated to Social Services that she was unfit to be a foster carer.

Lee spent some time at his parents' home, but the threat of physical abuse by his dad remained until he finally put an end to it. When Lee was 14 his dad started to hit him on his bare stomach with a belt. Lee decided that he wouldn't take it anymore. He got a saucepan and hit his dad over the head. His dad was unconscious for 15 minutes. His dad never tried to hit Lee again after that.

Lee appealed his expulsion from Mansea Hall. He hoped that in the appeal he could tell his side of the story, but once again the deck was deliberately stacked against him. The Board of Governors took six months to hear his appeal and then questioned him about what he had been doing for the six months that he was out of school. It was their fault that he had been out of school for six months, yet they used that fact against him. Lee knew of students who had been expelled for really bad behavior and were reinstated on appeal. He thought this would be the result of his appeal, but it was not. The boys who were reinstated were better at writing. They had a chance of doing well on the GCSEs, but Lee did not. His appeal was denied and Lee could not return to Mansea Hall. He was heartbroken.

Lee's Life After Leaving Mansea Hall

After Lee was expelled from Mansea Hall he was placed in several children's homes, each on a temporary basis. He did not like these placements and he asked his social worker to place him in another boarding school. After a few months, Lee's mum told him that he had been offered a place at a boarding school. It was a boarding school for children with special needs. He really wanted to be at a boarding school rather than in a children's home and he thought to himself, "Thank God for that."

The school at which Lee was placed was near Somerset, about 150 miles from London. It was nothing like Mansea Hall. It was not really a boarding school at all. It was not even much of a school. Mansea Hall had an elegant school building in which 50 boys were housed. The classes were held in the same location and some of the same staff that interacted with the students during the day were present at night. The new school didn't have an elegant building. Indeed it didn't have a building at all. The students were boarded in separate private houses, about three students to a house. There was a residential social worker in each house who closely supervised the students. The new place was more like a children's home than a boarding school. The school itself consisted of a few caravans, located far from where the students were housed. Lee felt that he had been lied to when he was told that this would be a boarding school like Mansea Hall.

Shortly after he arrived at the school, Lee was taken to an office to meet with an administrator. The administrator was not a teacher. He told Lee how he was expected to behave and that each time his behavior was found unsatisfactory he would get a black mark. If he got three black marks he would be transferred to a farm run by the school. While staying at the farm he would not be taken to movies or taken on other outings and he would have to work with the animals. Lee was so unhappy with the house and the school that he quickly accumulated three black marks, hoping that the farm would be better.

Lee expected a farm to be large and to have lots of pigs, cows and horses and fields to grow vegetables, but this farm was tiny and had just a few animals. The farm was really isolated and Lee saw no hope of running away. The ground floor of the farmhouse included a large kitchen, a large living room with three shabby sofas and a staff room for the residential social workers. The bedrooms for the staff and students were on the first floor. There was a fence with a small wooden gate a few yards from the house. Two pigs and four or five chickens lived in huts on the other side of the fence. That was the whole farm.

Lee liked the animals at the farm better than most of the people that he met at this so-called boarding school, and since the animals were pigs, that doesn't say much for the people. The pigs were kind of old and big and weren't very active. They would just lie down and let you stroke them. Lee fed them leftovers from the meals that the people had eaten.

Sometimes Lee was the only kid at the farm. At other times there were kids sent to the farm from the main boarding school for two or three days as a warning, to scare them into behaving. Being sent to the farm might work as a punishment if you had friends that you would miss at the school or if you enjoyed excursions to the cinema, to the bowling alley or to the ice rink. Lee didn't have friends at the main school and he didn't care for any of those activities. He liked it at the farm.

One day Lee's mum came to the farm for a visit. A social worker brought them into the living room. After the social worker left, Lee and his mum were the only ones in the room. The room was cold and the coal bin was empty. Lee threw a few of the cushions from the shabby sofas into the fireplace. They made a nice fire. His mum kept telling him not to, but they were still cold so he just kept throwing cushions into the fire until there weren't any more, except for the one that his my mum was sitting on. "Too bad the sofas are so big," Lee said to his mum. "I would have thrown them in too."

Lee and his mum both had a good laugh, the only time he got to laugh while he was at that boarding school and farm. After his mum's visit ended, one of the residential social workers went back into the living room and Lee went back in as well. The social worker noticed that all but one of the cushions that had been on the sofas, about a dozen of them, were missing. She asked Lee where they were. He just said, "I don't know."

One of the residential social workers took a dislike to Lee for some reason, possibly because he was well liked by the other staff. He didn't particularly like her either. One evening around 10pm she told him to go to his room. He told her that he didn't want to go to his room yet. She said, "Don't make me have to drag you to your room."

She started pulling him. He allowed her to pull him up the stairs, but when they reached the first floor landing he started to pull away. She lost her grip on his arm and the force with which she had been pulling him caused her hand to hit her face and made her lip bleed slightly. She accused Lee of assaulting her and went into the staff room and called the police. The situation reminded Lee of when his primary school teacher falsely accused him of pushing her down the stairs. "Why does this always happen to me," Lee wondered anxiously.

About 20 minutes later, a police car pulled into the driveway with screeching tires and flashing lights as if it were rushing to a bank robbery. Two police officers came into the farmhouse. The woman who had called them had been standing around in the living room, chatting with another member of staff. Just before the officers entered the room, she sat down on the floor, holding her hand over her mouth and crying. "I was trying to get him into his room and he swung at me and hit me in my mouth. He punched me in my face," she said to the officers, through her phony sobs. "I don't want him around here anymore."

"I never touched her," Lee said. "She did it to herself."

The police ignored Lee's side of the story and arrested him for grievous bodily harm. An officer grabbed Lee's arms, put them behind him and handcuffed him as he cautioned him. Lee was upset and angry about the woman's lying. They brought him to the police station, where they took his fingerprints and a DNA swab. Lee was charged with common assault and released on bail. The boarding school was still responsible for him and after several hours two security men sent by the school walked into the custody unit to pick him up.

"Do we need to hold you or will you be good and not try to run?" one of them asked in a threatening tone when they got outside. "We advise you not to run because we'll have to get heavy on you."

"I won't run," Lee replied.

They drove Lee to another house.

"You're going to be staying with us at this isolated house for a week or so," one of men explained when they got to the house. "Then your social worker will decide what to do with you."

"They'll probably put you in a secure unit for your own safety," the other man said.

"What's a secure unit?" Lee asked.

"It's a place where they lock up dangerous criminals and crazy people," the security man replied.

Lee was really worried about being locked up in a secure unit.

"Why can't I go back to the farm?" Lee pleaded.

"You assaulted a member of staff at the farm and now you're here with people you won't be able to assault," he replied. "Now go to your room and stay there."

Lee was desperate to get away, but they watched him constantly. One of them sat outside his bedroom door at night and one of them even sat outside the door when he went to the bathroom. All of the windows had security locks and the front door was always locked. Lee phoned his mum and asked her to come and see him. Somerset is far from London and she arranged for Social Services to pay for her ticket. She visited Lee at the house where he was being held. He told his mum that he was very unhappy about being kept at that isolated house and that he didn't want to stay there. As she was leaving the house, Lee told the men that he was going to see his mum off at the station. His real plan was to get on the train with her and that's what he did. He stayed at his parents' house in London and didn't return to the farm.

Lee had to return to court in Somerset three months later, although he was now living in London. There were no witnesses and the court took the word of the residential social worker over Lee's description of what had really happened. He pleaded not guilty, but the court found him guilty. Lee was required to meet with the Youth Offending Team in London once a week for a year. The false accusation by the residential social worker at the farm did a great deal of damage. The assault charge stayed on his record until he was 18 and caused police to treat him as a possibly violent person.

At 15 Lee felt that his plans for the future were finished. He knew that he had missed out on too much schooling and that he could not do well on the GCSEs. Lee was not willing to return to school. School had not worked out for him. He was unable to do well on writing assignments because of his undiagnosed dyslexia. Reading aloud in class had led to ridicule by the other students.

Lee at 16

When Lee turned 16 he was allocated a tiny studio flat by Social Services and he began receiving £40 a week from them. He remembers that the hallway in the flat was so narrow that although he was slim he had to turn almost sideways as he walked through. Cleanliness was important to him and he was glad to see a washing machine in the kitchen. The flat had a small bathroom with a shower and toilet. There were no windows in the flat except for a small one high up in the hallway.

Lee was looking for a relationship. He wanted to be with someone he could love and who would love him, someone whom he could trust. Not having any money left him with few options. Because he was only 16 he could not go to a gay bar and he didn't have access to online dating. He often rode his bike in central London around the different parks. It was in Green Park where he noticed a man looking at him, which was not unusual. The man's name was Patrick and he was in his early thirties and was quite attractive. Lee and Patrick dated for a while and Lee really liked him. He was interested in being in a relationship with him, but Patrick told him that he wasn't ready for anything serious. Lee was really disappointed because he thought that they were on their way to being in a relationship.

Patrick knew that Lee was struggling financially and asked Lee if he had ever thought about escorting. He told Lee that he was really good-looking and that he could make lots of money escorting. He offered to help him put his profile on a gay web site. Lee did not have computer access so Patrick offered to get his messages and to give his phone number to people who wanted to reach him. Lee was hesitant. The £40 from Social Services was not enough to live on. He wanted a regular job, but he was too young. He went to his long-time friend Shirley for advice. He thought that if he told Shirley that he was thinking of escorting she would say, "No, don't do it."

Instead, Shirley told him that she knew someone who had done escorting and had made a lot of money and that with Lee's looks he would be very good at it. With Shirley's advice he decided to accept Patrick's offer to put his profile on a gay web site. Patrick took pictures of Lee for the profile and posted it. There were many responses and Lee agreed to dates with a number of men. His first experience escorting was with a grubby, middle-aged man. He felt so dirty that he had to shower and scrub until his skin was red. He used two bottles of shower gel and even used some bleach.

Lee did not like the way things were going. He felt that he was meeting clients who were horrible people, people who wanted everything they could get from him for the £100 an hour that they were paying. He felt dirty, cheap, nasty, vulnerable and used. He knew that escorting on his own at his age was dangerous. A client could overpower him and force him to do things that he didn't want to do. A client could be a crazy person. He had heard of escorts being drugged and he refused drinks when he was with a client.

The greatest danger for an escort in London at that time was contracting HIV. Lee was very careful and made sure that his client was wearing a condom. On at least three occasions, however, the client removed the condom without Lee's knowledge before penetrating. When Lee discovered this afterwards he became was quite angry and confronted the client. One client tried to reduce Lee's anger by assuring him that he was not positive for HIV, but Lee was still concerned. Lee was tested for HIV several times. Fortunately, he never contracted HIV.

Meanwhile Patrick told Lee that he had changed his mind and wanted a relationship with him. One day Lee noticed on Patrick' computer that a cute-looking guy had responded to Lee's profile, but before Lee could reply to that guy Patrick had deleted the message. Lee realized now that Patrick was only passing messages to him from people who looked unattractive and was deleting messages from anyone who looked attractive. He saw that Patrick was trying to control him and would not allow any competition. His plan was to keep Lee in the background in case he wanted him later on. After that Lee did not want to see Patrick anymore.

Lee met a man named Stefan while escorting. He saw Stefan as a client four or five times. He liked Stefan and thought he could be in a relationship with him and Stefan agreed to this. Lee stayed with Stefan at his flat for several months. Although they agreed that they were in a relationship, their only interactions were sexual. They didn't engage in conversations. Stefan had a nice flat in Soho, an expensive sports car and a motorbike. Lee did not have to do escorting while he was staying with Stefan. He had a place to stay and his immediate needs were taken care of. Stefan, however, didn't give him extra money.

After a couple of months Stefan decided to go to his villa in Spain. Lee couldn't go with him because Social Services wouldn't get a passport for him until he was 18. Stefan stayed in Spain for two weeks. On returning he told Lee that he had had sex in Spain with another boy. Stefan thought that Lee would be okay with that, but Lee felt betrayed. He began to realize that his relationship with Stefan was not real, at least on Stefan's part. Stefan had only told Lee that they were in a relationship so that he could avoid paying Lee for his time as an escort, which would have been very expensive for Stefan considering how much time they spent together. Lee could no longer regard Stefan as his partner.

Lee had made around £4000 escorting, but it made him feel dirty and horrible. For the first time in his life, however, he was able to buy the food and clothing that he needed. Still, Lee hated every minute of it and wanted it to be over. He stopped escorting. He was pleased that at least he now had nice clothes so that he could go out and meet people.

After giving up escorting, Lee met a man named Larry at a gay club. They enjoyed each other's company and liked to watch "Absolutely Fabulous" together. Lee thought that Larry was in love with him. About that time Lee was running short of money and he asked Shirley for a loan of £80. Shirley knew that Lee had some jewelry and she suggested that he leave his jewelry with her as security for the loan. This was disappointing to Lee. He thought of Shirley as a close friend and thought that she should have trusted him without his having to leave his jewelry with her. He let Shirley hold about £1000 worth of jewelry as security for the loan of £80.

Lee told Larry that he was having difficulty trying to live on only £40 a week and that he was thinking about escorting again. Larry did not fully understand Lee's situation. Larry had an education and could get a job, but Lee's formal education had been interrupted and he had a record of juvenile offenses. Larry told Lee that if he started escorting it would end their relationship. Lee did not like anyone trying to control him and he broke up with Larry.

When Lee had the money to pay Shirley he went to her and asked to have his jewelry back. Shirley said it was gone. She had pawned it. Lee was shocked. He could not believe that a friend of six years would betray him that way. He realized later that for someone who had little money, having all that jewelry was just too tempting and he later reconciled with Shirley.

During this period, Social Services limited Lee's contact with his sister and his two youngest brothers. He could see them only once a year for a few hours. Social Services claimed that Lee would be a bad influence, based on the false accusations of violent behavior in Lee's record. It was only years later when they observed the way Lee improved his youngest brother's behavior that they could see that they were wrong about this. Lee was, and continues to be, the best influence in his siblings' lives.

Lee's siblings were not treated well in care. As is often the case, the foster parents favored their own children and the foster children were bullied by the other children. Lee's two youngest brothers left their care homes and returned, without authorization, to living with their mother.

Lee was 17 when he met George at a gay club. They started dating and soon went into a serious relationship. George became his partner and they are together to this day. George told Lee that people like Shirley and Beatrice were using him and Lee began to see the truth in that. George was a good-looking muscular man four years older than Lee. He both looked and acted tough and the toughness was real. People were afraid to challenge him even if they thought they had safety in numbers.

While Lee and George were visiting the house where Lee's mum and dad lived, a gang of around 20 thugs, mostly from the travelers, came up to the house. Some of them were swinging nunchucks. They wanted to beat up Lee because he wouldn't join their gang. George went outside and said, "What's your problem?"

One of them answered, "We don't a problem with you. It's Lee that we're after."

That was exactly the wrong thing to say to George. They didn't know that Lee was George's partner. George answered menacingly, "If you have a problem with Lee then you have a problem with me."

The thugs were afraid of George and left. Unfortunately, they did what cowards often do. They looked for someone weaker to assault. Lee's dad was going to the shop a few days later and was attacked by those thugs. He was badly beaten and had to go to the hospital. Lee was very angry about what the thugs did to his dad and thought about getting even. His friends asked him why he cared when his dad had physically abused him for years. Lee's answer was, "He's still my dad and I love him."

Lee's mum called the police. They wouldn't do anything. They said, "We know who they are, but we advise you not to press charges because they have firearms and we won't be able to protect you if there are any repercussions."

Lee asked the police why people in England who were armed illegally weren't arrested and put in prison. They had no answer. Lee wondered whether he was still in England or in some third world country. When Lee told Brian about this years later, the reaction of the police to the travelers reminded him of the police in *Pirates of Penzance,* who marched around bravely singing "Tarantara" until they heard that there were pirates abroad and then scattered in terror.

The travelers continued to harass Lee's family. They drove a stolen car into their driveway and got out and kicked the street door. They also rammed the door with a motorbike. Lee's mum was terrified. Lee told her that she needed to move out of her house to get away from them. The housing authorities would not arrange for her to move. They wanted her to pay first for damage that his dad had done in the house and for damage that the travelers had done. Lee and George were still in a one-room studio flat. His mum gave up her house and with Lee's two younger brothers moved in with Lee and George. It was obviously quite crowded. They had two cats and the cats ran away. Lee's mum was eventually rehoused in a permanent council flat.

Lee and George had no money. George was from Bosnia. He did not yet have his leave to remain and he wasn't allowed to work in the U.K. Lee suggested that they could do escorting on a temporary basis. They wanted to make enough money to start a business so that they wouldn't have to do that anymore.

Brian's Early Years

Brian's childhood was very different from Lee's. He was born in 1936, toward the end of the Great Depression. He grew up in Brooklyn, New York. He has some early memories of living near Brighton Beach, mostly unpleasant memories of sand being everywhere in the apartment, even in his food. To this day he hates beaches. He was extremely shy, even as an infant. If someone he didn't know came to visit he would scream so much that the visitor would have to leave.

Brian's father was quiet and reserved much like Brian, but unlike Brian he was not especially shy. Brian's mother was quite the opposite. She was outgoing and liked to be the center of attention. Once at a live show at the Radio City Music Hall a performer on stage sang, "It had to be you." The ending of the song is, "With all your faults I love you still." After the singer said "still" Brian's mother shouted out "dead" loud enough for the whole audience to hear. Many people in the audience laughed and turned to see who had called out "dead." On another occasion they were at a show at a hotel in the Catskill Mountains. One of the performers was playing the piano. Brian's mother shouted out, "You've got white keys and you've got black keys. Why are you playing in the cracks?"

When things like that happened Brian was extremely embarrassed and felt like hiding under his seat. His father, perhaps accustomed to his wife's antics, asked her why Brian was acting so disturbed. She answered in Yiddish. Brian had not learned Yiddish and his parents spoke Yiddish when they didn't want Brian to understand. Perhaps the first Yiddish expression that he learned was *Er schämt sich*, which in that context means, "He is embarrassed." (That's the German spelling but they used that expression in speaking Yiddish.)

Brian's family would be regarded as middle class or even lower middle class. Although his father was a pharmacist, he did not own his own drugstore and his salary was modest. Brian lived with his parents and a sister in a two-bedroom apartment. It was in a modern building with just over 100 apartments. It had a nice lobby and two elevators that could be used to reach the grocery store, drug store and other shops in the basement.

Brian always had sufficient food and clothing, although he was a bit unhappy with the clothes that his mother bought for him. He thought they were too old-fashioned. When he was around 10 his parents transferred him to a religious school, a yeshiva. He hated it there and did not do well in his studies. His mother, whose father had been a prominent rabbi, thought that attending a yeshiva would make Brian more religious, but it had the opposite effect, causing Brian to reject his religious heritage completely. After a couple of years at the yeshiva his parents allowed him to return to a public school.

Brian showed a talent for writing even in junior high school. It was in high school where he demonstrated a strong interest in academics. He excelled in all subjects except physical education. He hated the required gym class and his father arranged for a doctor's note to get him out of that class.

Brian had one sibling, his sister Rachel. She was five years older. They had the usual brother-sister squabbles as children, but they did many things together. They created a four-page newspaper for their apartment building. They even secured advertising from local merchants. They bought a mimeograph machine and worked together to produce copies of the paper. Mimeographing was a bit messy and they kept getting their hands covered with ink.

It is true that there is an element in the Jewish culture that values making money and this has led to an unfortunate stereotype, but there is another element in the culture that values scholarship. Scholarship was important to Brian and Rachel, to the point of competing for high school grades. Of course Rachel was five years ahead, so Brian was not competing with her directly, but was competing with her record. Scholarship continued to be important to both of them throughout their lives and they both became professors at top universities.

Brian's extreme shyness kept him from speaking clearly. People said that he mumbled. Guidance counselors mistook this for a speech impediment, but it was not. They sent him to a speech therapist who had him go through some tedious speech exercises that he found quite annoying and which did not help at all. The impediment was his painful shyness, not a problem with forming speech sounds. Although he was at the top of his class academically, his high school would not recognize this because they did not want him to give the main commencement address. They denied him the top academic award and made him a runner-up instead. This mistreatment by his high school remained a bitter disappointment for much of Brian's life.

Brian tried to avoid socializing while in high school, but he was somehow convinced to find a date and go to the senior prom. Someone arranged for him to take a girl named Sari. On his way to pick her up he imagined how the introduction would go:

"I'm Brian."

"I'm Sari."

Fortunately it didn't go that way. He bought a corsage for her and tried to pin it on her without stabbing her. He has no memory of how the rest of the evening went and he hopes that she doesn't either.

Brian disliked high school and schemed to graduate as quickly as possible. He even misled a guidance counselor into believing that the curriculum changes she was approving would allow him to graduate in the expected four years, but they actually allowed him to graduate in three and a half years. He entered Brooklyn College in 1952 at the age of 16. He did not do as well there as he had in high school. His greatest strength was in writing and he was easily at the top of his class in English composition. He read slowly, however, and although he was good at absorbing what he read, he could not keep up in classes that required large amounts of reading. He received low grades in those classes. He happened to have the same instructor in both an English class and a history class and that instructor expressed to him his disappointment that he went from being the top student in his English class to performing poorly in his history class. Some freshman and sophomore classes met in the late afternoon and Brian was caught sleeping in several classes.

Brian had few friends in college. He did not socialize and did not take part in any extra-curricular activities. A guidance counselor talked to him about this but that made little difference in his behavior. He was persuaded to join a house plan, a fraternity-like organization without pledging or initiation. The main obligation was to attend parties, something Brian found especially unpleasant. He was expected to socialize at the parties and he didn't know how. He was expected to like girls and he didn't know why. Brian dropped out of the house plan in less than a year.

Some people like to compare their behavior and style of dress to characters in movies. It was years later when Brian saw a movie in which the main characters acted and dressed like he had in high school and college. Unfortunately the movie was *Revenge of the Nerds*.

Brian was the prototypical nerd, although he didn't know what a nerd was at the time. He wore horn-rimmed glasses and he was extremely awkward socially. And of course he had a pocket protector. His dad wore one at work in the drug store and brought one home for Brian, which he wore proudly at school.

Brian knew what career he wanted from childhood. In the sixth grade he was asked to write an essay about his occupational goals and he wrote that he wanted to be a professor. During his freshman year at Brooklyn College he knew that he wanted to be a scientist and he needed to decide on what field of science he should enter. Biology was out because he would not consider dissecting a frog or any other once-living creature. Physics was out because he had been falling asleep in his first math class and had not followed the course material. (He later completed advanced math courses successfully.) He decided to study either geology or psychology. He liked his first geology class, although he did fall asleep in that class a few times. He also liked his first psychology class. The only thing that he remembers from a lecture in that class was a student describing something he had experienced the night before. The student began with, "While I was laying in bed."

Another student interrupted with, "lying in bed."

A third student said, "How do you know what he was doing it bed?"

Brian didn't care much for the lectures but he was fascinated by what he read in the text. He went on to take a laboratory class in experimental psychology. In the weekly four-hour labs the students worked in pairs preparing and running assigned experiments. Sometimes one student in each lab group would serve as a subject and sometimes one of the students would bring a friend to the lab to be a subject. The students in the class analyzed the results of their experiments and wrote reports. Brian found running psychology experiments extremely satisfying and easily decided that he wanted a career in experimental psychology.

Brian received low grades in a few courses that had a high reading demand, such as a history course in which students were required to read volumes of original source documents. He still had been able to maintain a respectable, but not exceptional, grade point average and he applied to several graduate programs. The University of Michigan Psychology Department had an unusual entrance exam. They relied on a test of interests, based on their research showing that this was the best predictor of success in a career in psychology. Brian did exceptionally well on that test, his interests matching those of students who later became successful in psychology.

At the age of 19 Brian moved away from his parents' home for the first time and stayed at a dormitory in Ann Arbor, Michigan for the summer. His roommate in the dormitory was a Christian Scientist. They got along quite well and Brian even went with his roommate to a Christian Science meeting. A year later he arranged to meet his former roommate and his former roommate's girlfriend for dinner. The former roommate told his girlfriend a story about how he and Brian had gone to a mattress shop while they were roommates at the dormitory, so that Brian could buy a bed for the apartment that he was going to rent. In his former roommate's story, Brian haggled with the salesman and got a much lower price than what the salesman originally quoted.

That was a gross distortion of what had actually happened. Brian wanted a high-quality mattress, but did not have enough money for the matching box spring so he bought a cheaper box spring. There was no haggling and no reduction in the price of either item. Brian suspected that his former roommate had told someone back home about having a Jewish roommate for the summer and that he had been exposed to the stereotype of Jews haggling over price. That was the last time Brian got together with his former friend. To this day Brian's concern about being stereotyped prevents him from negotiating prices even when that would be completely appropriate.

The dormitory housing was open to graduate students during the summer only. At the end of the summer of 1956 Brian, who had just turned 20, had to find other housing for the school year. Having been raised in a Jewish neighborhood in Brooklyn, he had not run into anti-Semitism before and his first painful experiences with this occurred in Ann Arbor. Trying to find housing, he was asked several times about his "nationality." A landlady seeking a roommate for another tenant who was not in town at the time told him that the other tenant had said she could select anyone she wanted, but she told Brian that she did not feel that she could select a Jew as the roommate for her other tenant. There was an opposite, but still disturbing, statement from another landlady who said that she preferred Jewish tenants because they were quiet and well behaved.

Brian finally was able to rent an apartment with the stipulation that he find two other graduate students to share it with. By the time he rented the apartment all of the graduate students that he knew had already made their housing arrangements for the year. He arranged instead for two undergraduates to share the apartment. He did not get along well with them. They took advantage of him, using and in some cases damaging some of the kitchen utensils that he had brought from home.

There was not much humor in the lectures that he attended as a graduate student, except once when the professor unintentionally said something hysterically funny. After a lecture on Freudian theory, the students had many questions about castration anxiety and the discussion went on for a while. The professor felt that the discussion had taken up too much time and said, "Let's cut it off now."

Brian was unhappy with the first year research assistantship that he had been awarded as part of his admission package. He expected to be helping to run a research project and instead he was made a subject in a psychophysical experiment. He spent 10 hours a week sitting in a dark room with three other people, pressing one of four buttons each time he saw a light in one of four positions. At the end of one of those two-hour sessions, the experimenter informed the subjects that the data was not useable because the light bulb had burned out. Yet the four subjects all were responding to the positions of the light flashes with accuracy well above chance. Brian knew that the positions of the flashes were determined by which of four shutters in the apparatus opened on each trial. He surmised that the subjects had, without awareness, associated the sounds of the shutter clicks with the positions of the flashes while the light was working and were responding to the sounds of the shutters after the light bulb had burned out. This assistantship did have a lasting benefit for Brian. He used the shutter click issue throughout his teaching career as an example of experimental error.

In Brian's second year in graduate school he was assigned as a teaching assistant in an introductory psychology course. His shyness and lack of spontaneity hampered his classroom teaching and he received poor student evaluations. When the instructor in charge of the course told him that he would not be renewed as a teaching assistant because of that he protested that his students were receiving higher scores on the final exam than those of the other teaching assistants. The instructor replied, "Anyone can cram a bunch of facts into the students," and that his job was to make them feel good about psychology courses so that when asked to donate to the psychology department after graduation they would be inclined to do so. That made Brian very cynical about teaching. He avoided teaching and concentrated on research for the remaining years of his graduate studies.

During Brian's last three years of graduate study he had five roommates at different times. He really liked one of these roommates and they became close friends. They planned a road trip together, but Brian was not accustomed to driving on country roads and at one point he had to pull to the right slightly off the pavement because of a large truck that was approaching in the opposite lane. When he pulled back onto the pavement his car went across the road and flipped over. Brian and his friend were taken by ambulance to a local hospital. Neither or them was seriously injured, but his friend was annoyed by the accident, which he blamed on Brian, and this damaged their friendship. Brian told his sister about the accident but he did not want his mother to know about it because she would be worried about him. He slipped up once a few months later in talking to his sister with his mother nearby. He said, "When I turned my car over," and then caught himself and quickly added, "for a new car."

Brian did not socialize much while in graduate school. He kept to himself and worked on his studies. His only companions were two cats that he had adopted as kittens from the same litter. He named them Frankie and Johnny. Other students regarded him as being something of a hermit and he knew that label was being applied to him. They wondered aloud about how he could be completing his graduate studies faster than other students. Brian's answer, which he never expressed to his fellow students, was that while they were out partying he was at home studying.

Writing the doctoral dissertation was not easy. Brian was good at writing but he had never before attempted to write anything that large. The real challenge, however, was the oral exam. A committee of four professors sat across from Brian in a small conference room, questioning him about the dissertation and related subjects. Brian was terrified. He squeezed himself into a corner of the room as if he were trying to escape into another dimension. At first he could barely recall his name, let alone anything about his dissertation. His dissertation advisor was one of the examiners and he was sympathetic and helpful. The moment that Brian remembers best involved two professors, a junior professor we shall call Jim and a highly distinguished professor we shall call Phillip. Jim quoted a statement in Brian's dissertation, saying in a pretentious manner that he disagreed with the statement and wanted Brian to defend it. Before Brian could answer, Phillip said that he remembered that statement and liked it. Considering Jim's junior status and Phillip's prestige, Jim was forced to withdraw his objection to the statement and he was better behaved during the remainder of the exam.

When did Brian realize that he was gay? It's hard to say. He knew from the sixth grade that he liked boys. He did not really understand why he enjoyed the sensations of a ruler being slid under his butt by the boy in the seat behind him in a classroom or of taking a knee to the butt from another boy. Homosexual preferences were not discussed openly at the time. Such preferences were hidden and kept secret. There was no World Wide Web. He did not know much about masturbation, but knew that he could produce an orgasm by leaning over the back of a sofa or on a filled laundry bag.

When Brian was 17 he came across an article by Max Lerner in the *New York Post*, "The Tragedy of the 'Gay.'" This was an epiphany for Brian. He finally understood what his feelings meant and that there were many other people with similar feelings. He also understood that those feelings were not accepted by most people and must be concealed.

During Brian's undergraduate and graduate studies, gay behavior continued to be hidden. The opportunities for a gay man to find companionship were very limited. There were a few gay bars in Manhattan when Brian turned 18 in 1954. They were hidden and often raided by the police. Two men dancing was considered a moral offence and could result in arrest. Compared to the present day, nothing really happened in a gay bar. The most men could do was exchange phone numbers. This was many years before the Stonewall uprising in 1969. Brian went to gay bars a few times with unsatisfactory results. He quickly gave up on trying to meet someone in that way. He had some interest in a gay friend, but that interest was not returned.

Gay pornography was hidden from sight and difficult to find. There were stores in Hollywood with shelves of straight porn VHS tapes in colorful wrappers, but gay porn tapes were kept under the counter in plain black wrappers. Brian found buying gay porn too embarrassing because the person at the checkout counter would know what he was buying. Looking back he wishes that there would have been automated checkouts at the time, but even when those were installed you couldn't always count on them for privacy. Many years later Brian was trying to run a package of condoms through an automated checkout at a drug store and the machine didn't read the item's code correctly. A clerk came over and as Brian waited at the checkout counter he heard over the loudspeaker, "How much is a box of 12 Trojan-Enz?" After that he bought condoms only on Amazon.

Brian just kept busy with his studies and later with his professional career. He did not have any sexual experiences with other persons while in college or in graduate school although he was strongly attracted to other guys. In looking back he understands that he had had several opportunities to get together with other guys, but he was too naive and he wasted each of those opportunities. There was a fellow graduate student named Harvey that he really liked. He rearranged the route of his next car trip to New York so that he could give Harvey a ride close to Harvey's home in Pennsylvania. As they approached the highway exit near Harvey's home, Harvey asked Brian if he would like to stay at his house overnight. Brian said no.

Why did he say no? The other student whom Brian liked was

probably coming on to him, but Brian was too naive to understand that. It was 1957 and no one even talked about gay sex unless they were making a homophobic joke. Later he realized that he had missed a great opportunity. He thought about what might have happened that night if he had said yes, but it was too late. He was beginning to understand the title of Lerner's article, "The Tragedy of the 'Gay.'" Brian was creating his own tragedies.

Brian's Early Professional Career

Brian received his Ph.D. four years after he entered the graduate program, but he had not received adequate career advice from the professors in his department. He hesitated to apply for teaching jobs because of the difficulty that he had experienced in lecturing as a teaching assistant in the introductory psychology course. Although he knew that he was good at research, he did not understand that research was the major component of academic appointments at top universities. He wanted to be at a university, but he thought that the best he could do was to work at a research laboratory.

As he finished his doctoral studies in 1960 and sought employment at a research laboratory, he understood that most laboratories held government contracts that required their scientists to have security clearances. He was still closeted and he knew that if it were discovered that he was gay he would be denied a clearance. The reason given by the government for denying a security clearance to a person who was gay was that this person could be a target for blackmail. The reason that person could be a target for blackmail was that they would be denied a security clearance if they were outed as gay. This nonsensical circular reasoning persisted through the 1960's and beyond. Although this form of discrimination gradually became illegal in most of the United States, it was not until 2020 that the Supreme Court ruled that a person could not be fired from a job just for being gay or transgender. Brian had kept his sexual orientation secret and he decided to take a chance and apply for a clearance, which was granted.

Brian's first job out of graduate school was at a university-affiliated research laboratory. While working at this laboratory he was assigned to visit a facility near El Paso, Texas, along with two other researchers. As they rode in a taxi in El Paso, the driver joked with one of the other men about how taxi drivers in neighboring Ciudad Juarez, Mexico would find you a girl if you asked them to. And then the driver said laughing, "Even a boy."

Brian saw this as a long awaited opportunity to have a sexual encounter with another person. That evening he walked across the border to Ciudad Juarez. It was a totally different world. The shops looked rundown, the streets were poorly paved if they were paved at all. There was an overpowering odor of raw sewage. Brian did something that he would never have had the nerve to do in the United States. He hailed a taxi and nervously told the driver what he wanted, *quiero muchacho*. The driver obliged and picked up a man in his early twenties and drove them to a hotel. The sex was very quick and not very satisfying, except that Brian felt that he had finally performed a sex act with another person.

After returning home from El Paso, Brian's preferred way of looking for escorts was to pick up hitchhikers along a boulevard that was known for such activities. He knew that looking for an escort in that way was dangerous. He also tried responding to ads in a gay publication. Meeting someone in that way would have been safer, but Brian wanted to see the person before committing to an encounter.

Brian picked up an 18-year-old named Darrell at night near the city center. Darrell was obviously looking for a client and Brian brought him to his apartment. Brian really enjoyed being with Darrell and there were several visits after that, about a week apart. Brian would leave his apartment door unlocked when he went to pick up Darrell so that they could get into his apartment quickly without neighbors observing them. Darrell must have noticed this. One night Brian went to pick up Darrell on a street corner as arranged, but he wasn't there. Brian returned home and Darrell was already in his apartment, but he was not alone. He had brought a friend and his friend had a gun. It was a homemade "zip gun." The two men were standing in his bedroom. All of the dresser drawers were open and Bryan saw a note lying on top of the dresser: "Don't try to f**k us up or we'll f**k you up." (Their note did not use asterisks.) Probably they had planned to leave before Brian returned.

Darrell demanded money and Brian gave him all that he had on him. Then Darrell asked Brian if he had a bank account. This made Brian very fearful. It was not so much that he feared the gun in the other man's pocket. He was too shocked to even think about that. He was in fear of being forever a target of extortion or of being outed as gay and losing his job and not being able to obtain another professional job. It was 1962 and even an unproven rumor that a person was gay could prevent that person from working as a teacher or even as a researcher. The professional status for which Brian had worked hard over a period of eight years would have disappeared.

Fortunately, Brian's fears were unfounded. Darrell explained why he had asked whether Brian had a bank account. Darrell was concerned that Brian would not have enough money to live on until his next paycheck after he had taken the money that Brian was carrying. Brian was greatly relieved by this explanation and believed that Darrell was not really a bad person and had come to rob him out of desperation. There would be no extortion. Darrell told Brian that his mother was being thrown out of her apartment because she owed back rent and that he needed to get enough money right away to pay what she owed.

As Darrell was getting ready to leave, Brian asked him, "Are you going to be able to pay your mother's back rent now?"

He replied, "No, I don't have enough yet."

Brian asked, "What are you going to do?"

Darrell replied, "We're going to rob a gas station."

Brian could tell from his demeanor that he really meant what he was saying. He thought about Darrell going with the other man and that man's homemade gun to commit an armed robbery. He pictured Darrell being shot by an armed gas station attendant or by the police. Although Darrell had robbed him at gunpoint, Brian still cared about Darrell. Brian's fear for himself was gone and was replaced by a fear for Darrell. Brian no longer saw himself as a victim and now he was able to take charge of the situation. This was easy to do because Darrell was clearly uncomfortable about robbing Brian. Brian told Darrell to send the man with the gun away and that he would get him the money that he needed to keep his mother from being evicted. Darrell now understood that he could trust Brian and he immediately told the other man to leave. With the other man gone, Brian drove to a nearby hotel with Darrell to cash a check. There were no ATMs then. He gave Darrell the additional money that he said he needed and drove him home.

Did Darrell really need that money urgently to save his mother from being evicted or was this a con? The next day Brian phoned the rental office for Darrell's mother's apartment. He knew

Darrell's last name and asked the rental agent how much was owed on her apartment. The rental agent told him that the amount owed had just been paid. Darrell had not been lying. Brian would have been willing to continue seeing Darrell, but Darrell thought that Brian would no longer trust him and their relationship ended. Brian wishes that Darrell had just told him about what he needed to help his mother and had not tried to rob him at gunpoint.

A few years later Brian picked up two young men who were hitchhiking. One of them was 18 or 19 and very attractive; the other was a few years older. Brian dropped them off at their apartment complex and they invited Brian to come in for a beer. The older man went elsewhere and Brian and the younger man went into the apartment. Brian started to approach the subject of doing something with him when a neighbor interrupted. The neighbor asked for a beer and sat down on the sofa and wouldn't leave. About 15 minutes later the older man returned and opened the apartment door quickly. He looked surprised that there was nothing going on. Brian left. Afterwards he realized what had just happened. The two hitchhikers were running a "badger game." The older man expected the younger man to get their victim into a compromising position. Then he would return and demand money. Extortion of a person who was gay was common at that time because most people who were gay were closeted and feared the consequences of being outed. When the older man returned to the apartment, however, he saw that their plan was ruined because of the unexpected intrusion of the neighbor. Brian was thankful that the neighbor came by when he did and that he just sat there and didn't leave. It saved him from being robbed or worse. Sometimes another person's obnoxious neighbor can be a good thing.

This experience did not stop Brian from picking up hitchhikers, but it made him more cautious about picking up more than one person. Several years later Brian picked up a hitchhiker on a boulevard leading to a beach. He was 19 and his name was Tim. Brian saw Tim regularly for about three years, even traveling with him to Las Vegas and Reno on separate occasions and staying at hotels there. After his experience with Darrell, Brian was reluctant to invite someone he was seeing to his house, but Brian trusted Tim and invited him a number of times. This led to some awkwardness with Brian's next-door neighbor who actually tried to chat with Tim once as he was leaving Brian's house. Brian told the neighbor that Tim was a student and even went as far as to loan Tim a textbook to carry on his way to his car to reinforce that explanation.

Of course Brian would never do anything with an actual student. A male student in one of Brian's psychology classes was coming on to Brian. It was so obvious that even Brian could see it. Brian would not do anything to encourage him, although he knew of straight male professors who had affairs with female students.

Tim asked Brian to hold on to the money that he had planned to give him until Tim asked for it. Essentially Tim wanted to build up some savings and Brian obliged. Brian liked Tim and told him that if he needed more money he could ask for it and he would not be asked to do anything in return. Brian didn't realize it at the time but in retrospect he may have had the incident with Darrell in the back of his mind and didn't want anything like that to happen again. Tim moved away after a while and they lost contact.

About six years later Tim phoned Brian and asked him to visit. He lived about 30 miles away. He said that he had converted to Christianity, but assured Brian that he would not be preaching to him. Brian visited Tim and after a while Tim asked if he could borrow $6000. He had been having a hard time financially and wanted the money for a car. Brian said yes but he didn't have his checkbook with him. He told Tim that he would mail a check and he did so the next day.

Brian didn't really expect the money to be returned. He hadn't given Tim much money while he was seeing him and he felt that Tim deserved a bonus, although not quite that much. A few months later Brian received a check in the mail from Tim. It was for $3000. Brian thought that was fair enough. Tim could have kept the entire amount. They had no further contact.

The city where Brian lived after he completed his doctoral studies was a long distance from where his parents lived and they did not visit often. Brian had never told his mother that he was completely ignoring the kosher rules that she had always followed. During one visit she was looking for something in his cupboard and saw a can of pork and beans. "What's this?" she said to Brian in a challenging tone.

"It's for the cats," Brian answered.

He didn't think that she believed him but they didn't discuss it further.

After three years at his first job, Brian accepted a position as the top researcher at a non-profit research foundation, but this position became less desirable after a change in management. By now he had two articles in prestigious journals and a colleague suggested that he apply for a faculty position at a new university campus in California. The university had not yet opened and Brian was spared the usual requirement of giving a job talk before an audience. He met only with the dean and associate dean. He knows that his lecturing ability was so poor at the time that if he had been required to give a job talk there would have been no possibility of his being offered the job. The associate dean was very positive about Brian's research accomplishments. He was hired and he moved to a city near the university.

As a new assistant professor, Brian's shyness continued to hamper his ability to lecture. He found a solution, however, perhaps an obvious one: Preparation. He prepared detailed lecture notes and reviewed them carefully before class so that he would not have to think about what he wanted to say while he was in front of the class. He also loved to mentor individual students, several of whom became established researchers. His success in mentoring was recognized by his colleagues and he received his university's top teaching award, which came with a heavy engraved paperweight. He joked about how he would like to throw it at the professor from his graduate studies who told him that he could never succeed in a teaching career. He used this award in a more serious way, counseling a graduate student after a professor had told her that she could not succeed as a teacher. He was already recognized as a successful teacher and he told her that she could be successful as well and that she should not be discouraged by what others told her.

There's not a lot more to say about Brian's relationships before he met Lee. His life was very lonely. He just kept busy with his studies and later with his career. He loved Frankie and Johnny and he wouldn't travel much because it upset them. Both cats reached the age of 16 and died over a period of a year. Brian decided that he would not get another cat so that he could travel.

Brian scheduled a three-month sabbatical in Denmark to work

with one of the leading scientists in his area of interest. At the time his parents had an apartment in Miami Beach and he visited them on his way to Denmark. Brian and his sister were concerned about their parents' financial situation. Their parents had not accumulated much savings and they were living mostly on Social Security, which paid very little. His mother wanted a nice apartment and most of their money went for rent. His father took a part-time job at a drug store. He couldn't be hired as a pharmacist because his New York license was not recognized in Florida. He did the work of a licensed pharmacist for the pay of a junior clerk.

When Brian and his sister were children their mother would sing the song, "Over the Hill," about elderly parents who had to go to the poorhouse because their ungrateful children wouldn't take care of them. Brian thought at the time that it was an attempt at indoctrination. When their parents were actually in need and Brian and his sister repeatedly offered to help, their mother didn't sing that song anymore. Instead she said that parents should be supporting children; children should not be supporting parents. Brian's parents refused financial help from him and his sister. They would accept gifts only for Mother's Day and Father's Day. Their family didn't observe Christmas.

Brian's First Visit To London

Brian stopped in London for a few days on his way to Denmark. He was aware that Earl's Court was a gay area and that a man who advertised massages there on a newsagent bulletin board could be expected to provide more than a massage. He looked at the notices posted at a newsagent near the Earl's Court station and called the number of a man advertising massages. The sex was okay but he was not particularly attracted to the man. The man who provided the massage told him that the place to find men looking to be paid escorts was Piccadilly Circus in central London. He went there one evening. There were some shops there, but all of them were closed in the evening. There was no obvious police presence, but it is likely that plainclothes officers were monitoring activity there. As many as a dozen young men were hanging around the area. This was in 1978. Piccadilly Circus is very different today and is no longer a cruising area.

Brian approached one man who he found especially attractive. He was tall and slim and had a nice face and body. His name was Harry. Harry agreed to go back to Brian's hotel with him. There was no discussion of the amount of payment and they took a taxi to Brian's hotel. The sexual experience was the best Brian had had so far in his life. This was not just because Harry was attractive, but also because Brian really liked him as a person. He gave Harry some money, which he later learned was double what he was expecting. Harry protested, "That's too much."

Brian was impressed with Harry's honesty. Brian had to return to Denmark, but he wanted to see Harry again and he got his phone number. Brian returned to Denmark and a few days later he phoned Harry to set up a meeting the following weekend. They arranged to meet in front of the Earl's Court underground station. Harry and Brian went back to Brian's hotel. Harry told Brian that he had been arrested at Piccadilly Circus. The charge was "loitering with intent." The police said they suspected him of intending to rob someone, but they knew very well what his intent really was. They just wanted a more serious crime. Harry and was due in court a few days later. Brian thought he was helping by giving Harry a large amount of money, but he learned later that this gesture backfired.

After Brian returned to Denmark, Harry, having much more money than he was accustomed to, decided to skip his court date and to travel to Scotland.

Brian tried to phone Harry again from Denmark but he couldn't reach him. Harry's flatmate answered the phone and told Brian that he had not seen Harry since Brian's visit. Brian was worried about Harry. He left Denmark a little sooner than planned and returned to London. He met with Harry's flatmate, who still did not know where Harry was. He asked around at Piccadilly Circus. Someone tried to steer him to a hotel where he supposedly would meet Harry, but fortunately for Brian he saw this as a robbery attempt and didn't go.

A few days later Harry returned to his flat and his flatmate told him that Brian was looking for him. He met with Brian and at Harry's request they travelled to Liverpool where Harry was from. Harry said he wanted to stay in Liverpool and would not continue to travel with Brian. Brian had been looking forward to spending some time travelling with Harry and he was extremely disappointed.

Brian returned to the United States the next day, stopping first in Florida where his mother was ill with cancer. He was sad because he thought that he would no longer be seeing Harry. His mother thought that he was sad because of her ill health and he felt guilty about leaving her with that false impression. As he left his parent's home in Florida, his sadness really was about his mother's illness. When his mother was younger she often had minor health complaints and could be regarded as being somewhat of a hypochondriac. Now things were completely different. She knew that she was terminally ill, but she never complained. She had been in bed during most of Brian's visit and as he was leaving she got out of bed and said to him, "I don't want you to remember me as lying in bed." She knew that she was dying and would never see her son again. Recounting this story still brings tears to Brian's eyes.

Brian had left his home phone number with Harry and Harry phoned him after Brian had returned to California. He was disappointed that Brian had left England. Harry hadn't really wanted Brian to leave. If there had been mobile phones available to them at that time Harry could have reached Brian before he left

England and they would have resumed their travels, but Harry had no way to reach Brian before Brian was back in California. They kept in touch by letter and sometimes by phone. This was of course before email and text messages. Brian arranged for Harry to receive a weekly payment so that Harry would not have to continue escorting to make money.

Harry told Brian after a few months that he didn't want those payments anymore because his friends resented his having money all the time when they didn't. Around that time, Brian received a disturbing letter from Harry's father, who had somehow found Brian's address among Harry's things. The letter asked why Brian was giving Harry money and what he was expecting from Harry in return. In a carefully worded reply, Brian indicated that he was trying to help Harry give up escorting and that he was back in the United States. He told Harry's father that he was not asking for anything from Harry in return. Harry's father replied to Brian's letter. He appeared to be satisfied with Brian's reply and his tone was much friendlier.

A few months after Brian had seen his mother in Florida, she needed more constant care than his father could provide and she was moved to a nursing home. Brian's father was with her as much as possible throughout her illness. In addition to keeping her company, he used his knowledge as a pharmacist to check on her medication. Brian's mother died at the nursing home. Brian's father called Brian and Rachel to inform them. Knowing that they were both teaching classes at the time, he discouraged them from travelling to Florida and said that he would take care of everything.

Brian visited Harry once or twice a year for a few years. They travelled to Ireland, to Italy and to Greece and stayed on Crete for a few days. As much as Brian liked Harry, the relationship was difficult. Harry was a heavy drinker and Brian had to deal with that. A few years later, Harry started to be more demanding, not like the first night when he said that his payment was too much. One day in autumn of 1981 Brian was at home recovering from hemorrhoid surgery. Harry phoned him and said that he needed some money right away. At that time it was necessary to visit a bank to arrange a foreign transfer. Brian didn't feel up to it and told Harry that he couldn't send anything that day. Harry said, "Are you blowing me off?"

Brian didn't like that. He did send Harry some money the next day. They kept in touch a while longer and Brian learned that Harry had become a carpenter. He was happy to hear that Harry was able to support himself without escorting. After a while they drifted apart and eventually lost contact.

Brian's father now lived alone in his apartment. He did not have much income and he still refused help from his children. His old small-screen TV had broken and Brian and Rachel decided to buy a new large-screen set for him as a Father's Day gift. They did not tell him about it. When it arrived he thought it was being delivered to him by mistake. He looked at the paperwork and realized that it was a gift and Brian and Rachel convinced him to keep it. He clearly enjoyed the new TV.

Less than two years later Brian received a phone call early in the morning. The man at the other end said that he was with the Miami Beach police. Brian had picked up a hitchhiker in Huntington Beach the night before and for a moment thought that the man on the phone had said Huntington Beach and that there was some trouble about last night. The man on the phone continued and told him that his father had died. Brian began to cry and it was a few minutes before he was able to call his sister.

Brian lived in California and Rachel lived in Arizona. They both made flight reservations immediately and flew to Miami. Brian took ground transportation to a hotel in Miami Beach and went to the rental car desk in the lobby. He was told that they had cars available only for people with reservations. Out of desperation, Brian learned a little trick that he has since passed on to other people. He walked across the hotel lobby to a phone booth, phoned the car rental company and made a reservation. Then he went back to the rental desk and told them that he had a reservation. They looked it up and he was able to get a rental car.

He met his sister that evening outside their parents' apartment. They had keys, but there was a police tape across the door. They called the police number on the tape and were asked if they were the only heirs. They said yes and the police said they could go in.

The next day they attended the funeral. The rabbi took a pair of scissors and cut Brian's shirt. Brian was a bit surprised, but he recalled the biblical custom that mourners tear their garments as a sign of grief. Brian and his sister spent the next day putting their father's affairs in order. This was much easier than it normally would have been because their father had left detailed instructions. He was a very meticulous person and didn't want his children to be burdened unnecessarily with details after his death. Brian and his sister returned to their homes after a few days.

One day a year later Brian was walking for exercise and about a 10-minute walk from his home he saw a black kitten climbing a tree. He didn't try to pet the kitten, but perhaps the way he looked at it gave the kitten the impression that he felt some affection for it. Something strange happened the next night. At around midnight Brian heard some sounds coming from his garage. It sounded almost like a baby crying. He opened the door between the kitchen and the garage and found a black kitten in the garage. He recognized the kitten as the one he had seen climbing a tree the day before. The kitten seemed to be hungry and came into the kitchen. Brian had no milk but he had some half and half and he put some in a dish and put it out for the kitten. He didn't want another cat so he left the kitten in the garage, which had an opening to the backyard, for the rest of the night. The kitten was still there the next morning. Brian advertised that he had found a cat, but there were no responses. On an intellectual level Brian did not want to have a cat. He knew this would keep him from travelling and he wanted to be free to travel. But emotionally he began to really love this cat. He named the cat Midnight because he was totally black and because he had found the kitten in his garage at midnight.

About a month later, Midnight disappeared. Brian was heartbroken. He put up signs and advertised and even went to see a cat that someone had found, but it was not Midnight. As weeks went by, he thought about almost nothing but his missing cat. Six weeks after Midnight disappeared he received a phone call from a woman who had found a cat in her garage. She told Brian that it had taken her several weeks to get close enough to the cat to read the phone number on his collar. That was Brian's number that he had taped to Midnight's collar. Brian went to the woman's address. Midnight was there and came over to him, but a car passed nearby and frightened Midnight and he ran off. Brian was afraid that he had lost Midnight again, but Midnight came back and Brian was able to get him into his car and to drive home.

When they got back to Brian's house, Midnight sat on Brian's lap and purred and would not leave there for many hours. The bond between Brian and Midnight was stronger than anything Brian had ever experienced before. Brian would not travel for more than two or three days at a time and didn't really like to be away even for that long. Midnight had access to the street, but he stayed mostly in the backyard, occasionally sitting in front of the house. He was never lost again. Brian and Midnight were together for 18 years. When Midnight began to lose bladder control, Brian covered his own bed with absorbent pads so that Midnight could continue to sleep there. One day Brian went out to do some grocery shopping and when he returned home he found Midnight lying stretched out and motionless, partially hidden under a bush in front of the house. Brian's best friend for 18 years was gone. Brian never got another pet.

Brian As a Professor

Brian's shyness and lack of spontaneity not only hampered his lecturing but also prevented him from advancing further in his career at the university. Although he had superior administrative skills, he was never considered for a position of dean or higher. He had twice been appointed associate dean, under two different deans. This allowed them to take advantage of his administrative skills without giving him a higher-level position.

One of Brian's duties as associate dean was to host luncheons for important visitors. He would pay the restaurant bill and the university would reimburse him. On one occasion he submitted the bill and was told that it was too high for the number of persons attending the luncheon. The university had a maximum allowance for luncheons based on the number of people attending. One morning Brian was in his office being interviewed by a student from the campus newspaper. Associate deans dealt with instances of students cheating and the topic of the interview was why students cheat. In the midst of the interview, Brian's phone rang. It was the school's business manager. He told Brian that he had a solution for the luncheon bill exceeding the allowed amount. Brian should add the names of three people to the list of those who attended the luncheon, even though they were not actually there. Brian didn't like that solution. The school's administrative assistant had a different solution. Brian should accept the reduced reimbursement and make up the difference by claiming that he had made a business trip to another campus and requesting reimbursement for the miles traveled. And we wonder why students cheat.

Brian was invited to the Vice Chancellor's home for dinner one evening, along with one other guest. He thought later that this might have been an audition for a higher-level administrative position. If it was, it was an unmitigated disaster. The conversation was exclusively small talk. They discussed some little café in Paris that was off the beaten track and similar things for hours. Brian had never learned how to do small talk. He sat in the Vice Chancellor's home all evening without uttering a single word. He was trying to think of something to say the whole time. He knew that he was expected to participate in the conversation. He knew that sitting there silently in the home of the Vice Chancellor, who was the highest-level academic administrator at his university, was not acceptable. His panic was overwhelming and made it even harder for him to speak. He had sweaty palms and his face was flushed, but every time he came up with something to say, the conversation had moved on before he could say it. He was not invited back.

Brian did not like to be the center of attention, but if he had to be, as in teaching a class or running a meeting, he was able to handle the situation. The one thing that saved his career was an appointment as the head editor of a prestigious journal. A friend who knew Brian's work recommended him for an appointment as an associate editor. This was a position in which communications were in writing and not face-to-face. Brian was good at this and rose to the position of head editor in a few years.

Brian was easily embarrassed and nervous about hiding his sexual orientation. Because of this some perfectly innocent events turned into potential sources of embarrassment. On one occasion he was at a scientific conference with a straight friend. Late at night his friend was complaining about having chapped lips and wanted to go to the drugstore. Brian had the rental car and drove him there. And what did his straight friend buy at the drugstore with Brian standing next to him? A tube of Vaseline.

On a visit to Istanbul, Brian's luggage was delayed and that night he realized that he needed a comb. He called the concierge at the hotel and asked if he could get him a comb. The concierge said there was one in the minibar. Brian was puzzled, but he looked in the minibar. There was no comb. There was a condom. Clearly something had been lost in translation. Brian took out a piece of paper and a pen and drew a picture of a comb. He went down to the concierge desk and explained that this was what he wanted. A comb was delivered to his room. He was thankful that the Turkish student who was showing him around was not there when this language confusion happened.

About two years before he met Lee, Brian had a stopover in London on his way back from a conference in Prague. It was 2002. He was 65 and planning to retire in a few years. He checked into a hotel and looked on an escort service's website for someone to see.

He thought that Vladimir looked good in his photo and his description said that he was 18 years old. He scheduled a meeting with Vladimir at his hotel. It was a very strange meeting. As soon as he arrived, Vladimir opened the minibar and took out a bottle of champagne, which he drank quickly. His face seemed a bit odd, but his body was okay and the sex went well.

As they chatted afterwards, Vladimir told Brian that he had gone to law school in Russia. This didn't make sense to Brian. If he was really 18, how could he have gone to law school? Vladimir admitted that he was not 18 and that the age in his description on the website was a lie. He was actually 26. That's why his face looked odd. It was not the face of an 18-year-old. He still insisted that the looked like an 18-year-old and he was offended if Brian didn't agree completely. Brian was surprised at the deception. The website had a reputation for providing honest information about their escorts. Brian learned later how Vladimir had been able to lie about his age on the website: He was having an affair with the owner of the site.

Brian would sometimes take an escort to dinner after they were finished at the hotel. They would go to a nearby restaurant and the escorts had always accepted Brian's choice of restaurants. This occasion was different. When Brian suggested going to dinner, Vladimir took out a list of the most expensive restaurants in London and selected a restaurant from that list. They took a taxi there and Vladimir ordered a meal with champagne and caviar. Brian paid the rather large bill and they left the restaurant. Then Vladimir said he wanted to go to another restaurant from his list. They took a taxi there and things were repeated: champagne and caviar and another large bill.

Brian was shocked by the way Vladimir was taking advantage. He should have known better, but he continued to see Vladimir on several subsequent visits to London. At a prestigious rooftop restaurant overlooking the Thames, Vladimir went through two bottles of champagne and ordered a third one. He told Brian how people had given him diamonds. The restaurant was noisy and Brian pretended not to hear him. As they were leaving, Vladimir lifted a waiter off the floor. Brian experienced a level of embarrassment that he had not experienced before, but he continued to see Vladimir and the embarrassment only got worse.

Vladimir wanted to go to Edinburgh and Brian went there with him by train. They started to check in at one of the best hotels, but there was a problem with their reservation. They were supposed to have a room with twin beds, but the only available room had just one double bed. The manager was concerned, but Brian heard the assistant manager, after looking at Vladimir, say, "They won't mind."

They were shown the room and Vladimir didn't like it so they moved to another hotel. That hotel had a twin room, but the embarrassment didn't stop there. Vladimir went down to the bar and Brian went to join him a little later. He found Vladimir with a man and woman in their thirties. Vladimir had already told them that he was with someone and when Brian arrived he told them that was who he was with. The couple was trying hard to show that they were very modern and accepted other life styles. They asked Brian questions such as, "How long have you been together." Brian wishes that he had answered, "too long."

On a later visit they traveled to Rome and did a lot of walking around the city. Brian complained that Vladimir was walking too fast and getting ahead of him. He said that friends should try to walk together to which Vladimir replied coldly, "We're not friends." Brian realized at that moment how foolish he was being, but he was not yet ready to give up on Vladimir.

Brian was trying to get Vladimir to slow down on his drinking. He learned that the only thing Vladimir liked more than champagne was expensive gifts. Vladimir wanted a very expensive laptop case that he had seen in a shop. He didn't actually have a laptop. Maybe that's what he was going to ask for next. Brian told Vladimir that he would buy the case for him if he stopped drinking for five days. Vladimir did so and Brian bought the case.

Brian wanted to visit Russia and thought it would be helpful to go there with a Russian-speaking escort. The trip did not go smoothly. When they arrived at the airport in Moscow, Brian had a very long wait at immigration. The other people waiting didn't form a queue as they would in London; they formed more of a mob. Brian had to push and shove his way through, using skills he had acquired from his early years in New York City. When he finally reached baggage claim, Vladimir was nowhere to be found. With his Russian passport he had gone through immigration quickly and had taken a taxi to the hotel. It was of course the most expensive hotel in Moscow. The next night Vladimir went out drinking on his own and came back to the hotel drunk. He was holding an empty bottle of champagne to his mouth upside down, trying to get the last drop out as he staggered around the lobby. Brian found this embarrassing, but he was glad it happened in Moscow and not in London.

During the next few days, Brian did get to see a few of the main sites of interest. He went to Saint Basil's and to the Kremlin, but without Vladimir who was drunk most of the time.

Brian had purchased tickets for a performance of *La Cenerentola* at the Bolshoi Theater prior to leaving London. The theater was across the street from their hotel and Vladimir went to the theater with him. An elderly veteran approached Vladimir and asked for a seat in their box, to which Vladimir agreed. Brian did not mind this and he enjoyed the performance.

Brian and Vladimir went out to dinner one evening in Moscow. The waiter asked Vladimir, "Would madam like to start with some hors d'oeuvres?" Vladimir replied indignantly, "I am not a madam." He was not in drag but he always looked that way.

Brian expected Vladimir to be helpful in making arrangement to travel on to Saint Petersburg, but he was too drunk to help and Brian had to make the arrangements on his own. Their cabin on the Russian train was so run down that Brian double-checked the tickets to verify that they were really in first class.

Vladimir's mother lived in Saint Petersburg. Brian was aware that she not only knew that he was working as an escort but was giving him advice about this. She told Vladimir that he shouldn't make Brian buy expensive meals so that Brian would have more money to give to him. Vladimir's mother rented a small flat for Brian and Vladimir. It was in an extremely rundown building, but at least it was centrally located. Vladimir's mother stayed in the flat with Vladimir and Brian sometimes. Brian suspected that Vladimir's mother had arranged with the renting agent to receive a cut of what he paid for the rental of the flat.

As in Moscow, Brian did much of his sightseeing in Saint Petersburg on his own. One day Vladimir's mother took Brian to the Winter Palace while Vladimir stayed in the flat, drinking as usual. Brian enjoyed the Winter Palace with its spectacular art collection. The next day Vladimir and Brian went to the Summer Palace by boat.

One evening Brian went with Vladimir and his mother to a nice restaurant where they had an enjoyable meal. After Brian paid the bill, Vladimir ordered a very expensive bottle of champagne. He opened it and decided that he didn't like it. The maitre d' demanded payment. Vladimir refused and he and his mother ran out of the restaurant and hailed a taxi. Brian would rather have paid for the champagne and avoided the embarrassment, but Vladimir and his mother were already getting into the taxi and the situation was out of his control. The maitre d' started chasing the taxi on foot but they got away. The next day Vladimir took Brian to a furrier's and looked at expensive mink coats, but Brian did not buy anything. A few days later, Brian and Vladimir returned to London.

After returning to London, Vladimir wanted to travel to Brighton and Brian agreed. He didn't bring his mother, who was back in Russia. This time he brought his sister. He learned that she was living with a man who she didn't like, but who was giving her money.

As Brian was preparing to leave for California, Vladimir asked him when he would see him again. Brian replied that he didn't know. Vladimir said, sounding annoyed, "What do you mean you don't know. When is your next vacation?" Vladimir was presuming that Brian would see him at his next opportunity. Brian returned to California and never saw Vladimir again.

Rachel

Brian's sister Rachel had married at a young age and had two children, Daniel and Solomon. She was very modern in some ways, good at using computers and comfortable with technology. In other ways she was a bit old fashioned, at least in Brian's view. She carried on her mother's religious traditions. She lit candles every Friday night, as did her mother before her. She would not write, use a computer or handle money on the Sabbath. She kept a strictly kosher home. Unlike her mother's older sister, Brian's beloved aunt Esther, she did not observe all of the Sabbath restrictions. She travelled on the Sabbath, turned lights on and off and tore things if required. She thought that her aunt was going a bit far tearing toilet tissue in advance for use on the Sabbath.

Unlike Brian's mother, his sister did not expect Brian to observe her religious practices. He followed the kosher rules when visiting in her home and when she visited in his home, but she did not object to his eating food that was not kosher when they dined at a restaurant. One thing that his sister did seemed especially old-fashioned to Brian. When she learned that her younger son Solomon was gay, she advised him to see a rabbi to have an arranged marriage.

Rachel's religious beliefs were sincere and deeply held. They led to behavior that was beneficent beyond any religious interpretation. When she was 19 years old she suffered a detached retina. At that time recovery required that both eyes be bandaged for two weeks. She was an avid reader and this short period without vision made her think of the plight of persons who were permanently blind and could read only the limited selection of books that were available in Braille. She vowed that when she recovered she would devote time to helping people who were blind and for the remaining 68 years of her life she did just that. She learned how to Braille, which at that time meant manually punching dots in a matrix for each letter. She taught others to Braille and it is likely that she was responsible for thousands of additional books being available to those without sight.

Over the years Brian looked forward to visits by Rachel and her husband Ruben. During one visit they took Brian to an opera in

Los Angeles. It was *Tosca*, starring Placido Domingo. They had excellent seats, close to the stage. Brian remembers his amazement at hearing the full quality of this great tenor's voice, something he had never been able to hear in recordings. On other visits they enjoyed eating at a Spanish restaurant overlooking the Pacific Ocean in Laguna Beach. They noticed that many guests at that restaurant during the summer were preparing to go to the Pageant of the Masters, which was within walking distance of the restaurant. In this pageant, famous paintings and sculptures are recreated with real people in costumes and makeup playing the roles of the people in the paintings and sculptures. In advance of their next visit Brian ordered tickets for the Pageant and for several years he went to the Pageant with his sister and her husband after having dinner at their favorite restaurant.

Brian and Lee's First Meeting

Brian scheduled a two-day stopover in London on his way home to California after teaching a summer course in Estonia. His hotel room at Paddington was plain but adequate. There was a king size bed and a small round table flanked by two armchairs. Brian had stayed there before. He would have preferred something a bit more luxurious, but he really liked the easy access to Paddington Station where he could catch the Heathrow Express to the airport. He also liked the anonymity offered by the direct access to the hotel's elevators from the station. He knew that he could arrange for someone to come to his room without any embarrassment on his part or on the part of his guest. He was looking for a sexual encounter, although he really yearned for something much more. He wanted an encounter that would grow into a genuine and lasting friendship.

Of course he knew that such hopes were quite unrealistic. He knew that one should not expect an encounter with a paid escort to lead to a genuine friendship. Indeed Vladimir, whom he had been seeing for two years, had told him rather bluntly that they were not friends. Yet there was still a spark of hope that he would find someone who might initially just meet his physical needs but who would become the genuine friend that he had been seeking all his life, a friend from whom he would not have to hide his sexuality.

Brian was 68 years old and had lived alone ever since completing his doctoral studies more than 40 years earlier. That night he decided to visit a gay brothel in the Earl's Court district of London. He had been to that brothel once before. His experience on his previous visit was mixed. On that visit, a young man approached as he stood near the entrance. Brian learned that the man worked there and he arranged to be with him. They went to a room at the brothel and Brian found the sexual experience pleasant, but then the young man, who apparently had an interest in film, started criticizing Michael Moore. Brian held Michael Moore's work in high regard and was quite annoyed by this. But he decided to visit the brothel again nevertheless.

Brian first went to the brothel's website which had photos of the men who would be working there that evening. It was hard for

Brian to understand how a brothel could be operating so openly in London. He saw a photo of a man who looked interesting to him. He took the tube from Paddington to Earl's Court and walked to the brothel. The man he was interested in was there, but when he inquired at the reception desk he was told that this man was just leaving and also that there were no rooms immediately available. He was asked to wait in the reception lounge.

The lounge had several comfortable high-backed sofas. There were three other men in the room. They were well-dressed older men and each was trying to avoid eye contact with the others. Brian felt quite uncomfortable and left. He returned to his hotel and took out a list of three escorts whose photos he had found on a gay website. The first name on the list, and the escort that he was most interested in from the photos and description on the website, was Lee, although he was using a pseudonym on the website. Brian decided to phone Lee.

"Why is your number withheld?" Lee asked in a challenging tone when he answered the phone call. Lee was suspicious of people who concealed their phone numbers when they called him.

"I'm at a hotel," Brian replied.

Lee was still concerned about Brian's number being withheld, so Brian gave Lee the hotel's number and his room number and Lee agreed to call him back.

Lee called right back as he had promised, satisfied that Brian was not deliberately withholding his phone number. They arranged to meet at Brian's room about an hour later. Brian had had previous encounters with escorts who did not look nearly as good in person as they did in their pictures on the web and he didn't really know what to expect.

Brian heard a knock on his hotel room door. When he opened it he saw an 18-year-old young man with the most beautiful face he had ever seen. He had striking brown eyes and a well-formed slim body. He did not look a lot like his pictures on the web. He looked much, much better. Brian secured the door and things proceeded as you might expect. We will not go into details. But afterwards, something happened that was far from expected, either by Brian or by Lee. They sat in the two chairs opposite each other at the table and began to talk. That part was not unusual for Brian. He usually would spend a while chatting with the person he had employed as an escort if he found that person at all interesting, and sometimes he would take them to dinner.

But this conversation was different. Lee was used to people just handing him money with no eye contact after sex and rushing to leave. As he and Brian talked, Lee felt that Brian was really interested in what he had to say. It was like catching up with a friend who he had not seen for a long time. He told Brian a lot about his life, even about how he had been sexually abused as a young boy. Now this could have been an act. Maybe Lee was just trying to get a bigger tip. But Brian knew that was not the case. He knew somehow that Lee was being completely sincere. Lee talked about how other clients had taken advantage of him and how he was trying to make money for a refrigerator and other items for his flat. Again, this could have been phony, but it was real and Brian never doubted that. He paid Lee the agreed amount and Lee left.

Although Brian had entered the encounter looking for sex and Lee had entered the encounter looking for money, each had a deeper need. Each needed a friend, a true friend. Brian needed a friend who would fulfill his physical needs but still would remain his friend. He needed a friend who would not reject him because of his physical needs. Lee needed a friend who would provide the financial support that he needed without making excessive demands and more importantly, would always show him respect. He wanted a friend who he could trust after having been let down by others who pretended to be his friends. This was never to be a sugar-daddy sugar-baby relationship, a type of relationship that each of them despised.

When did Lee and Brian's relationship change from client and escort to friends? The feelings that grew into a great friendship were present even from their first conversation, sitting across from each other at the table in Brian's hotel room. Lee was reluctant to trust people right away, yet he told Brian about being sexually abused as a young boy. Why would an escort tell something like that to a client? It made sense only if Lee was already beginning to see Brian as someone he could trust and who would be his friend. When Brian thinks back about that first conversation he recognizes that he was already deeply in love with Lee.

The rest of the night and the next day, Brian could not stop thinking about Lee. He had only one more day in London. He had never before called an escort two nights in a row, but it was extremely important to him to see Lee again. It was not so much that he needed another physical encounter so soon. It was mostly out of concern that Lee might allow other clients to take advantage of him because of his immediate need for money to purchase necessary items for his flat. Brian phoned Lee that evening and Lee came to Brian's room again. Once again there was a sexual encounter and a long conversation in the two armchairs. They agreed to meet again when Brian had his Christmas break later in the year. As Lee left, Brian handed him a sealed envelope containing more than three times what he would usually have been paid. Brian wanted to cover Lee's immediate needs and reduce the urgency of his escorting.

Years later Brian regretted not having gone further. He regretted not offering Lee sufficient financial support so that he could stop escorting immediately, but this was something Brian did not think of at the time. He was not yet ready to make such a commitment and Lee was certainly not ready to suggest anything like that so early in their relationship. It is also possible that Brian understood that the decision to stop escorting had to be made by Lee. He did make that decision within a year and Brian was glad that he did.

Surprisingly, Lee did not yet realize the strength of Brian's feelings for him even after the second time Brian called him. He was uncertain about whether Brian would see him again after that, although the signs of Brian's attachment to him should have been obvious. Lee did not want to start trusting someone too soon, having been burned repeatedly in the past. Some people had just enjoyed his company once or twice and didn't call him again.

Their First Trip

Brian and Lee kept in touch by phone for the next five months. Brian was still teaching and could return to London only for the Christmas break. He stayed at the same hotel and arranged for Lee to meet him there. They had made plans to go to Spain, first to Barcelona and then to Granada and Madrid. When Lee arrived at the hotel room he made a call to his mobile phone provider. He was angry and swearing loudly. Brian had not seen him like that before. Harry and Vladimir had talked that way at times when they had been drinking and Brian asked Lee if he had been drinking, but he hadn't been. Lee felt that the mobile phone company was being unreasonable and had disrespected him. Brian did not expect Lee, who had been so quiet and polite with him, to be capable of such anger, but Lee did become extremely angry when he felt that someone was taking advantage of him. This outburst of anger with the mobile phone company did not affect his interactions with Brian.

Before leaving for Spain, Lee insisted on getting something from his flat that he had forgotten to pack. It was a piece of a blanket that he had kept with him at night from early childhood. It was the proverbial security blanket. It reminded Brian of Linus's blanket in the "Peanuts" comic strip. This might have seemed childish to Brian, but it did not. Instead it deepened Brian's feelings for Lee. In the same hour in which Lee had shown a level of anger in a phone call that shocked Brian, he now demonstrated a genuine sensitivity and vulnerability that Brian had seen in him in their first two meetings. Brian did not yet fully understand the depth of his feelings for Lee nor did Lee understand this, but an incident the same night, after they arrived in Spain, made this clear to both of them.

They flew to Barcelona that evening and checked into a luxury hotel. After a few hours Lee said that he wasn't feeling well and wanted to go home. Brian tried to talk him out of it. It was already late and Lee would not have been able to get a flight until the next morning. Brian did not want to return to London with Lee. He wanted to continue his planned trip to Granada. He had long been fascinated with the history of the Alhambra and really wanted to see it. Why should he ruin his plans because of an unreasonable companion that he barely knew? That was his rational response to the situation, but his emotions took over and tears streamed from his eyes. He had never experienced such intense emotion because of a companion wanting to leave. It was obvious to Brian when he recalled that incident later, just as when he recalled their first conversation, that he was already deeply in love with Lee.

Seeing Brian's reaction, Lee agreed that he would not leave. Now Brian was so relieved by Lee's agreement to stay that his crying became even more intense, causing Lee to say to Brian that if he didn't stop crying he really would leave. Brian tried to stop crying. Lee said, "I think you're crying because if I leave you won't want to see me again."

Brian replied, "I would want to see you, but I wouldn't." In retrospect Brian realizes that was not true. He would have wanted to reconcile with Lee even if Lee had left.

Lee stayed with Brian at the hotel in Barcelona. The next day he noticed a large tower just outside the hotel entrance. It was a station for a cable car that went high above Barcelona to a nearby park. Lee wanted to go on the cable car, but Brian was acrophobic and didn't even want to go up in the tower, let alone to ride in a cable car that ran high above the city. Lee would have gone on the cable car ride alone, but Brian's desire to be with Lee every minute led Brian to agree to go on the cable car.

They took the elevator in the tower to the level from which the cable car departed. Brian was already terrified just from the height of the tower, but he wanted to be with Lee and he was ready to get into the cable car. He planned to sit on the floor of the cable car and to not look out. Lee saw that Brian was terrified before they even got into the cable car and he told him that they could forgo the cable car ride and go down to the street and walk together to the park instead, which is what they did. Lee could have insisted that Brian go on the cable car with him but he did not. This gesture of kindness on Lee's part meant a lot to Brian and is something he never forgot. Brian was greatly relieved when they reached street level. He really enjoyed their stroll to the park.

Two days later they went on to Granada as planned. They both enjoyed their visit to the Alhambra. Lee especially liked the ceiling mosaics and took pictures of them. They had a long conversation in their hotel room that evening, covering a wide range of topics. Brian was impressed with Lee's intelligence and told him so. Lee responded that no one before had told him that he was clever. The hotel was in a rather old building and Lee, who believes in ghosts, felt uncomfortable walking through the corridors. He asked Brian to walk through the hotel with him and they walked up and down the corridors until Lee felt more comfortable. Having been able to do this made Brian very happy.

The next day they took the train to Madrid. Brian had been to Madrid before and wanted to see Picasso's *Guernica* again. Although Lee did not care for museums at the time, Brian persuaded him to accompany him to the Museo Nacional del Prado. They went inside, but got separated because of the ticket queue. After purchasing the tickets, Brian couldn't find Lee. He started to think that Lee had gone back to the hotel because he didn't want to go to the museum and he phoned the hotel room, but there was no answer. Although Brian should have known that Lee wouldn't have just left him at the museum, he became extremely upset. But then Lee showed up in front of the museum. He had used a different entrance and had been looking for Brian. Brian realized that he had been foolish thinking that Lee had gone back to the hotel without telling him.

Now that Lee had joined him, Brian asked at the museum information desk where to find Picasso's masterpiece. Oops! They were at the wrong museum. Brian had forgotten that the painting was not at del Prado, but was at the Museo Reina Sofia. Fortunately that was just a short walk away. They went there and saw the painting. Brian told Lee that this was the only painting that had ever had made him cry. Smaller reproductions did not have the same emotional impact and he was glad to see the actual painting again and to show it to Lee.

Back in London

A few days later they returned from Spain and checked into a luxury hotel west of central London. It was two days before Christmas. Brian stayed at the hotel while Lee joined his family for the holidays. Lee returned to the hotel after Boxing Day.

It was difficult at first for Lee to believe that Brian was someone he could trust, someone who really loved him and would always care about him. He had had many bitter disappointments as a child and as a young adult. He thought that Brian's affection might be real, but he had been burned so many times that he was not ready to believe that Brian could be trusted completely. When he had attended a school or stayed at a children's home, staff members had told him that they were his friends and that they loved him and he wanted to believe that. But once he left the school or children's home he never heard from them again. When he was escorting, many clients, including Brian, told him that they loved him, but all the others had nothing further to do with him once they got what they wanted.

Brian and Lee were in a hotel suite that had a separate bedroom and living room. Early in the morning on the day they planned to check out, Lee woke up and saw that Brian was not in the bedroom and that Brian's clothes and luggage were not in the room. Lee called Brian's name in a plaintive, questioning voice that Brian had never heard before. Lee thought, maybe for just a moment, that Brian was like the other people who just used him and left. But Brian had not left. He had moved his things into the living room so that he could start packing without waking Lee. When Lee came out of the bedroom and saw Brian in the living room, he said, "I thought you had gone." Lee still sounded quite troubled but Brian didn't understand why. He didn't know yet about the people who had used and abandoned Lee, even from an early age. Brian wishes that he had said something reassuring to Lee at the time, but all that he said was, "I just came out here to pack."

Even after more than 17 years Lee and Brian still remember that incident. Brian did not fully understand what had happened until many years later. He had never given a thought to sneaking out of the hotel that morning while Lee was still asleep. Maybe he should have done that with Vladimir. When Brian learned years later about how other people whom Lee had trusted had let him down, he understood how Lee could have thought, for just a moment, that Brian had left. Brian still remembers the pain in Lee's voice when he called his name in a questioning tone, thinking that Brian might have left. Although Lee would certainly not blame Brian for that incident, Brian still feels badly about causing even the briefest of pain for someone that he loves so much.

We are intrigued by characters in fiction who combine toughness with vulnerability. Lee was like that in real life. As a child he was friendly and easygoing. People took advantage of him, but this did not change him at first. The change came when he was unjustly expelled from Mansea Hall, the boarding school that he loved. The staff, administrators and students who had acted like his friends while he was at the school were suddenly gone. They did nothing to stay in touch or to help him through the difficult period that followed his expulsion. He was thrown into an ugly world of prostitution. He had to develop a hard shell for his own protection, just as any beautiful creature in nature would have to develop. He would not allow anyone to disrespect him and he would get even with anyone who did not treat him properly. His vulnerability still came through, but only to those who cared to see it. Brian could hear it in his voice the day when Lee had thought that Brian had left the hotel without him.

Less than a year into their relationship, Brian agreed that he would provide Lee with a fixed monthly income rather than pay him for his time. They had already moved away from a client-escort relationship to a relationship of friends and that agreement put a final end to the previous type of relationship. What made it possible for their relationship to transform is that it was always based on complete honesty. Brian knew that Lee wanted financial support. There was never any concealment of that. Lee knew that Brian wanted physical contact and Brian didn't expect Lee to pretend to be attracted to him.

There were some incidents that highlighted the transformation from a client-escort relationship to a relationship of friends. One night Lee and Brian were staying at a hotel in Brussels that had a private gym. Lee came to their room and said that he had just been exercising at the gym. Brian asked Lee if he had showered. That was a big mistake. Lee was compulsive about cleanliness and was offended by Brian's question. He had already showered at the gym but he showered again in the room. Later that night Brian said he wanted to have physical contact and Lee refused saying, "You asked me to shower and I'm not going to shower again, so I won't do anything with you."

Brian was shocked by Lee's rejection and by the reason that Lee gave for it. This almost led to a breakdown in their relationship. Seeing just how affected Brian was by his rejection, Lee agreed that he would be willing to do something after all, but it was too late. Brian's shock was so great that he was unable to do anything with Lee for the two days that remained in his trip. But although there was no physical contact, something else happened the next evening that had a lasting impact.

Lee invited Brian to his flat for dinner. Brian had never been there before. They had always met in hotels. Lee was an excellent cook and made spaghetti bolognese. Brian remembers this as the best meal that he had ever had. The food was great, but it was the company that made the meal so memorable. Lee had a piano in his flat and played Beethoven's *Fur Elise*. Brian was a Beethoven enthusiast from childhood and considered Lee's playing to be outstanding. So even though there was no physical contact that evening, Brian's feelings for Lee were becoming even stronger. He had to return to his hotel to prepare for his trip home the next morning. As soon as he got on the tube to head for his hotel, even though he had left Lee only a few minutes before, he began to miss Lee sorely.

Brian preferred to be alone with Lee and in the first few years of their relationship that was straightforward. Brian stayed at hotels and Lee would visit him there. Brian did not insist on luxury hotels, but he would not stay in the cheapest ones either. Lee began to understand that Brian's resources were limited and that the hotel bills were a drain on his resources. He realized that Brian was spending a lot on hotels while he was not able to afford items that he wanted for his flat. Lee suggested that Brian stay at his flat some of the time while he was visiting in London, sleeping on the sofa bed in the living room, but there was an obvious difficulty. Lee was living with George in a one-bedroom apartment. Brian was reluctant to stay with them and Lee agreed that he would ask

George to stay at an inexpensive bed and breakfast for a few nights while Brian was staying at their flat. The difference between the bed and breakfast charge and what Brian would have spent at a hotel would be available to Lee to buy items that he needed for his flat. George was not happy with this arrangement. He didn't see why Brian couldn't save the same money by staying at a bed and breakfast himself rather than at a moderately expensive hotel, but he went along with the arrangement because that's what Lee wanted.

One night while Brian was staying at Lee's flat they argued about something. Neither of them remembers what it was about, but it became rather heated. Lee said he wanted Brian to leave and that he would drive Brian back to his hotel. Brian said that he didn't want to leave and he refused to get up and go to Lee's car that was just outside the door to his flat. You might think that this would have made Lee angry but it had the opposite effect. Lee explained that he needed to know if Brian would stay with him even after they had argued. Lee felt that other people in his life had abandoned him when things got difficult. He realized now that Brian was not like that and that Brian really loved him. Certainly they had arguments from time to time over the years, but Lee understood that Brian would never abandon him no matter what happened and Brian understood that Lee would never abandon him.

One might think that Brian and Lee were becoming partners, but there was no possibility of that. Lee made it clear from the beginning that the time he could spend with Brian was limited because he had a partner. This situation was quite awkward for Brian. He understood that he would never be Lee's partner and he accepted that, but his interactions with Lee's partner George were difficult from the start. Their first interaction, if one can call it that, occurred when Lee and Brian returned from a trip to the continent on Eurostar. At the time the London terminal for Eurostar was at Waterloo. As Lee and Brian exited the controlled area of the station, Lee said goodbye to Brian and looked for George. When Lee and George saw each other they simply walked off together without saying anything to Brian. Lee was not ready yet to introduce Brian to George and Brian was not ready for that either.

Lee in College

As Brian learned more about the way Lee was treated in primary and secondary school and about the interruption in his education, it saddened him greatly. He could see that Lee was as intelligent and motivated as any of the university students with whom he had worked, but that an uncaring educational system had so far prevented him from achieving a status in life appropriate to his intelligence and motivation. Brian wanted to help make up for what that system had done to Lee, but his expertise was in mentoring university students and he did not know how to help someone who had not finished high school. Without fully realizing it, Brian was trying to fit Lee into a mold that was familiar to Brian, but was not a good match for Lee. He thought that Lee's goal should be entering a university and he looked into what steps would be required to accomplish this.

Lee told Brian about his problem with spelling and Brian, with his background in psychology, understood immediately that Lee was dyslexic. He knew from his teaching experience that dyslexia should not be a bar to higher education, but that some accommodations were needed. In almost all of the large classes that Brian had taught he would receive a note from the university's learning center informing him that a student in his class would need to complete exams at the learning center. At the learning center the student could use a computer running a voice recognition program and would be given additional time to complete exams. Brian made an appointment for Lee with a psychologist in London so that he could be tested for dyslexia and the results showed that he was indeed dyslexic. Brian convinced Lee to enroll in a college program for students who had not been able to complete the exams that are usually required for university admission. Lee was reluctant to do this, but he could see that it was important to Brian and he agreed.

Lee entered this program at a local college and he conscientiously attended classes four days a week. Brian hoped that Lee would see that he could hold his own with a group of students who were studying to enter university and Brian believed that this was accomplished. His history teacher was impressed with his knowledge of the origins of the Church of England, which Lee had learned about from the many documentaries that he watched on television. Indeed his preference for educational television programs had placed him well ahead of his fellow students in general knowledge.

Brian helped Lee prepare a PowerPoint presentation that he gave in front of the class. Lee had been reluctant to speak in class because of his earlier bad experiences in school. He had had difficulty reading aloud in his primary and secondary schools because of his dyslexia and that had led to ridicule by other students. Lee's presentation at his college was well received by the teacher and by the other students. Brian was really proud of Lee when he made this successful presentation and Lee was happy with this accomplishment. Lee successfully completed the university preparation course and received a certificate that allowed him to apply to universities.

Chrissy and Tiger

Lee wanted a pet dog. He still had a need to feel safe after his encounters with gang members who lived near his mum's house. His flat in London was in a somewhat rough neighborhood and there had been an attempted break-in. He decided to get a German Shepherd who he named Chrissy. Brian met Chrissy the first time he visited Lee at his flat in London. She was a very cute and affectionate dog and was very protective of Lee.

Lee 's flat did not have a back garden and Chrissy was indoors except when taken for walks. When she was about two years old, Lee purchased a male German Shepherd so that Chrissy would have some company. He named him Tiger. Tiger was very large and scared Brian the first time Brian encountered him in Lee's flat, but that was quickly resolved when Tiger saw that Brian was Lee's friend. Lee was very close to his dogs. He liked to take them to parks and beaches where they could run free. He took excellent care of them, keeping them well groomed and free of fleas and ticks.

When Lee was 19 he learned that his youngest brother Christopher, who was 13, was in trouble with the police. Christopher was involved with a gang and was accused of burglary. He was out of control, not going to school, staying out late, smoking weed and refusing to tell his foster parents where he had been. All of his foster placements had failed because of his behavior. He was due in court in a few months and it was likely that he would be placed in a secure facility, because Social Services would not be able to find a foster home willing to take him with his record of bad behavior and breakdowns of placements. Lee didn't want that to happen to his brother and he asked Christopher's social worker if Christopher could be placed with him. She was reluctant to place a 13-year-old with a 19-year-old brother. Part of her reluctance was due to a homophobic belief that living with a gay older brother would make the younger brother gay. There were no good alternatives, however. The social worker could see that Lee was a responsible person who was taking care of himself and was not into drugs and she agreed to the placement on a trial basis. Lee was living in a one-bedroom flat.

He bought a single bed and put it in his living room for his brother.

Christopher had been smoking weed and cigarettes and had not been eating properly. He was skinny and gaunt-looking when he arrived at Lee's flat. Lee got Christopher to give up weed and cigarettes and to return to school. He made sure that his brother was well fed. The social worker was pleased with the improvement in Christopher's appearance and behavior and gave a favorable report to the judge when Christopher went to court. Because of the improvement in his behavior that Lee had brought about, Christopher was given a conditional release with only the requirement that he wear a tag for a few months. The judge told Christopher that without Lee's help he would have been put into a secure facility and that he should thank Lee for his freedom. Christopher lived at Lee 's apartment for two years. His improved record with Social Services allowed him to be placed with a foster family and he made the change, expecting a foster family to be less strict than his older brother.

Lee in California

During the first five years that Brian was seeing Lee, Brian always travelled to England to visit him. Lee expressed an interest in coming to California and Brian was interested in that as well. They arranged a visit in April 2009. In earlier years Brian would have offered Lee only an economy or at best a premium economy ticket from London to Los Angeles, whereas Brian always travelled in business class. By the fifth year of their relationship Brian was fully committed to the idea that Lee deserved the same comforts and luxuries that he enjoyed and Brian provided a business class round-trip ticket, using his frequent-flyer miles as he did for all of his own trips. Brian met Lee at the airport in his 2006 Lexus. They had already determined that Lee would do the driving on the way back to Brian's home because the only available flights arrived in the evening and Brian did not drive after dark. This was also a necessary arrangement because Lee became physically ill in cars when he was not the driver.

Brian was still going to his university for student meetings although he had already retired. Lee needed a car to drive when Brian was away and they went to a storefront office of a major automobile rental company in a nearby strip mall. The only car available was a small underpowered Japanese import. Lee had wanted to drive a more powerful car in California. He had been limited to driving underpowered cars in the U.K. because he was under 25.

Two days later they went to a Whole Foods market for dinner. They both liked the self-service hot food and salad bars there. As soon as they got their food and sat down Lee told Brian that he was planning to leave the next day. Brian had expected Lee to stay another week. As they sat down to eat there were tears streaming down Brian's face. Brian's reaction to Lee saying he was leaving was just like his reaction to this in Barcelona. While Brian was crying uncontrollably and trying to hide this from people at nearby tables, Lee said to him, "You don't even care that I'm leaving." Through his tears, the only thing Brian could think of saying was, "You think I have something in my eye?"

Lee had become unhappy with the visit. He wasn't used to being away from George for so long. Also Lee's asthma was acting up. He was still smoking at the time and the cigarettes seemed to be stronger in the United States. It was the height of the pollen season and the asthma medicine that he was able to get differed from what he was accustomed to.

Lee was willing to put up with those things if Brian really wanted him to stay. Lee did know why Brian was crying. When he said that Brian didn't care about his leaving he really just wanted Brian to tell him that he did care. Seeing that Brian was devastated by the thought of his leaving so soon, Lee agreed that he would stay longer. Brian understood that Lee didn't like the rental car that they had gotten at the strip mall and he wanted Lee to have a rental car that was more to his liking. They drove to LAX where they could find a much larger selection and rented a Mercedes C-Class. Brian drove this once and liked the smaller size compared to his Lexus.

Overall they had a very enjoyable visit, including a trip to San Diego. Lee would have liked to go to San Francisco or Las Vegas by car, but Brian was seriously acrophobic and he did not want to go anywhere by car that involved mountain passes. Brian took Lee to his university and showed him the laboratory and office where he worked, something Lee really appreciated. There were some arguments. Lee liked to play loud music and Brian was concerned about disturbing his neighbors.

Lee was scheduled to leave on Sunday the following week. On Friday Brian went to the university for a scheduled meeting with students. When he returned home, Lee told him that he wanted to leave right away. Brian pleaded with him to stay until Sunday as planned, but at Lee's insistence he called the airline to see if there were any frequent flyer business class seats for that day. There were two flights that day on the airline on which Lee was ticketed. A seat was available on the next flight, which was leaving in a little over one hour. No seats were available on the later flight, leaving in four hours.

Lee demanded that Brian drive him to the airport immediately. Brian refused, saying that there wasn't enough time for Lee to get to the airport and board the earlier flight. Lee thought that he would have been able to get to the airport in time for the earlier flight and that Brian was delaying him because he didn't want him to leave. He left Brian's house and started driving towards the airport in the rental car, but he turned back after a while. He was angry about Brian's refusal to drive him to the airport, but he was not serious about going to the airport on his own.

Brian agreed to get Lee to the airport for the later flight, although there were no frequent flyer seats available. Lee told Brian that if he could not get on that flight he would stay in a hotel in Los Angeles rather than return to Brian's home. Brian drove to the airport and parked close to the terminal for the airline on which Lee was ticketed. They went inside and Lee asked the ticket agent if he could switch to the next flight. But the next flight had no frequent flyer seats available to which Lee could switch. As they were leaving the terminal, Lee expressed concern that their relationship would be ended by this conflict about his departing early, but that thought had never even occurred to Brian. Brian began walking back to his car in the parking garage and Lee walked with him and got into the car. That was a moment of great relief for Brian. He had believed that Lee would not come back with him and would stay in Los Angeles instead, but that was something that Lee had said in anger and didn't really mean.

There was considerable tension between them on the ride back from the airport. Less than half way back they stopped at a gas station. Brian had been driving but Lee wanted to drive because of the way he felt ill when someone else drove. This was aggravated by Brian's tendency to brake as soon as he saw brake lights ahead, whereas Lee's style of driving was to ease into a stop when the vehicle in front stopped. Brian refused to give Lee the key, which Brian kept in his pocket. It worked by proximity, so the car would not start unless the key was in the car. Brian stepped out of the car and would not return. Lee told Brian that he had found a scratch on the glove compartment door and that he wanted Brian to look at it. Brian moved part way into the car to do so and Lee, knowing that the key worked by proximity, started the engine. Brian moved out of the car, but once the engine was started the key was no longer needed and Lee started to drive off.

Brian walked to a nearby pay phone and pretended to make a call. He wanted Lee to think that he was calling the police, something Brian would not have done. Lee drove up to where Brian was standing and let him in the car on the passenger side. He told Brian that he would drive to Brian's home. He entered the freeway, but the car's navigator was still set to LAX and he entered in the wrong direction. Brian realized this immediately and told Lee that he was going the wrong way. Lee didn't believe him. Brian insisted that he wanted to get out of the car. Lee pulled into a truck weighing station that was closed at the time. Brian got out of the car, but there was nowhere to go so he got back in. Lee left the freeway and re-entered in the correct direction. They drove to the Whole Foods Market to get something to eat and then back to Brian's house.

Then something happened that Brian will never forget. Lee still believed that his insistence on leaving that day and the hostility that he expressed towards Brian when Brian refused to drive him to the airport for the earlier flight had ruined their relationship. Because he really believed this, he was concerned that Brian would no longer give him monthly payments and that he would need time to adjust to this. He asked Brian if he would give him one more monthly payment before he stopped those payments. What Brian said in response he regards as probably the most spontaneous thing he had ever said. He didn't think about how to respond to Lee's request. His words came straight from his heart: "I would never do anything to hurt you."

It had never occurred to Brian to end his financial support for Lee. Lee could see that Brian would not abandon him because of an argument. He already knew this, but bad experiences that he had had with other people in the past had made him fear that it could happen. Brian was still deeply in love with Lee. The argument about Lee leaving early didn't change that at all. They watched a movie together that night and Lee left as scheduled two days later.

Their First House

Brian visited Lee in London two or three times a year. He stayed at a hotel and Lee would visit him there. Brian would bring sandwiches and soft drinks and they would enjoy a leisurely afternoon and evening. Lee would ask Brian before he came to the hotel if he should bring a change of clothes. This was really a question of whether he should be prepared to shower at Brian's hotel. If Brian said yes, Lee would take this as an indication that Brian wanted to do something sexual. During those years Brian was giving Lee a set amount of money to live on so that Lee would no longer need to do escorting. Brian began to understand, albeit slowly, that he wanted to do more for Lee than just provide him with enough money to live on.

Lee really wanted a house and Brian realized that paying for hotels on his visits was wasteful. There was a more immediate reason for purchasing a house. Lee was living in a rented flat with his two large dogs and some neighbors were complaining about the dogs barking. The rental agent told Lee that he would have to rehome the dogs or he would be evicted. Brian also cared about the dogs and wanted Lee to have a house with a large backyard. There was another important reason why Brian wanted to buy a house jointly with Lee. He had heard about one of Lee's brothers becoming homeless and he wanted Lee to own a house so that no matter what happened in the future, Lee would never be homeless.

At first Lee thought that Brian could afford to buy a house for him and George and a separate house for himself. Lee later realized that this was not the case. He agreed that if Brian bought a house, he and Brian would stay there when Brian visited and the rest of the time he would stay there with George. This had the same awkwardness of George being asked to stay at a bed and breakfast when Brian visited, about three months a year.

Brian made some inquiries by phone about obtaining a mortgage. He was shocked to learn that he was not eligible for a mortgage in the U.K., even with his substantial retirement income, because he was over 65 years old. Brian had considerable retirement savings and he began to think about using these savings to buy a house in the U.K. It was when Lee told Brian that he was about to do some redecorating at his London flat that Brian finally decided to tell him that he was prepared to buy a house.

Brian returned to California and left it to Lee to find a house within their limited budget. Lee selected a house in a small village about 5 miles from Herne Bay. It was a two-story end-of-terrace house. On entering the house you would see a staircase just to the left and a blank wall to the right. A door to the living room should have been there, but previous owners had closed it off, presumably to have more wall space in the living room. The kitchen was straight ahead. It was quite old-fashioned with a linoleum floor and wallpaper. It included a built-in fridge-freezer and a built-in dishwasher. A door on the right at the far end of the kitchen led to the living room. Entering the living room, there was a glass door to a conservatory on the left. The conservatory was not especially well built and had a door to the back garden. The back garden was quite large, perfect for the two large dogs, and the conservatory would be their indoor doghouse. The living room was quite long and had bay windows at the end towards the front of the house.

When they moved to the new house, Lee put off his goal of entering a university. But Lee had not really adopted that as his goal. It was actually Brian's goal. Fortunately Brian came to understand that Lee was not one of his undergraduate students, devoted to academic studies and concerned only with moving on to higher education. Lee had told Brian what he really wanted to do, but Brian hadn't listened properly because what Lee wanted to do was so unfamiliar to him.

Lee did not want to go to university. He wanted to do property development. From childhood he had a passion for doing creative work with his hands. He liked to take things apart to see how they worked. He often made repairs for his friends and family. He was never paid for that but they appreciated his efforts. Although they may have been using him, the experience that he was gaining and his creativity gave him a foundation for the work that he would do in property development.

When Brian and Lee took possession of the house it was barely livable without considerable redecorating. Paint was peeling off the walls in the front room, the upstairs floors were in poor shape and there were no window coverings. There was a small w/c in poor condition under the stairs on the ground floor. The shower in the first floor bathroom did not work well. When Lee and Brian arrived at the house they had no beds yet. They slept on a mattress on the floor in the front room. But Brian thoroughly enjoyed staying there with Lee while Lee made improvements to the house. Lee's partner was still at their old flat and Brian was pleased to have some uninterrupted time with Lee without George being asked to stay at a bed and breakfast. Lee worked hard at fixing up the house over a period of six months. He plastered and painted the walls, put in new floors and renovated the upstairs and downstairs bathrooms.

While living at that house, Lee decided to quit smoking. It was difficult because he had started smoking at a young age. It took several attempts, sometimes using patches, but he finally was able to quit completely. Brian was really happy that he quit.

About three years after Brian and Lee moved into their house, Brian invited his sister Rachel and her husband Ruben to visit for a few days while they were travelling in the U.K. on vacation. After Brian had invited his sister to visit, he and Lee had a very heated argument. They do not remember how it started. Lee told Brian that he didn't want to see him anymore. Brian might not have believed this, knowing that it was said in anger, but Lee went on to make an exception to his not wanting to see Brian. He said that Brian could be at their house while his sister was visiting, but aside from that he did not want to see Brian anymore. A few minutes later Brian said to Lee, "Even if you won't see me anymore I will still love you."

Lee's response was, "You're making me feel bad."

Brian had said that he didn't want to see Lee anymore out of anger during an argument and although he didn't really mean it, he included the exception about Brian's sister's visit to make what he had said seen more real. Lee knew that without that exception Brian would not have believed that Lee was really telling him not to visit anymore. Less than an hour later, Lee said, "Let's go do our shopping." As they drove to the supermarket, the anger and the argument disappeared and their relationship was back to normal.

Brian had never told his sister that he was gay, although she probably had figured it out. He was not ready to have his sister meet Lee. Lee agreed that he and George would stay elsewhere while Rachel and Ruben were visiting. He had told Rachel about

Lee, saying only that he took care of the house when Brian was back in California, that he was an expert at renovations and that he had made many improvements. Brian was afraid that Rachel would suspect that there was more to Brian's relationship with Lee if she saw how young and attractive Lee was. Ruben admired the work that Lee had done in the house and said, "You're lucky to have found him."

Brian thought to himself, "You have no idea how lucky I was to have found him," but he didn't say it out loud. Ruben played with Chrissy and Tiger in the back yard, but Rachel was afraid of the big dogs and would only watch them through the glass door between the living room and the conservatory.

Brian wanted Rachel and Ruben to meet Lee on a future visit, but that did not happen. Sadly, Brian received a phone call from Rachel while at home in California several years later that he had imagined he might receive one day: "Brian, I need you."

Ruben had died unexpectedly. It was too late to get a flight to Phoenix that night so Brian flew out the next morning. He stayed at a hotel near Rachel's house for several days. Daniel, Emily and their daughter Marcy stayed at Rachel's house while Solomon stayed at a motel. Brian returned to California after the funeral. From that time he phoned Rachel every Sunday morning.

Brian enjoyed playing with the dogs when he visited Lee. He brought each of them a wooden dumbbell toy on several visits. He would throw each toy across the backyard. Tiger would run and get his toy, bring it back and put it down and Brian would throw it again. Chrissy would get her toy, bring it back and keep it in her mouth. She may have been concerned that if she put it down, Tiger would get it. Still it was great fun for Brian, and probably for Chrissy and Tiger, to play in their backyard.

During his visits, Brian would accompany Lee when he took Chrissy and Tiger for walks. One day they were walking in a field near Lee's house and Brian couldn't find the path through the hedges that Lee and the dogs had taken. Lee sent Tiger to find Brian. Tiger came back to Brian and led him to the path through the hedges. That amazed Brian. He had not realized until then just how intelligent the dogs were.

Lee loved the two dogs deeply. They were both affectionate to him, although Chrissy demonstrated her affection more explicitly, rubbing against his hand or foot whenever she was near him. He recalls how he selected her from a litter. He noticed that the owner of the litter would call the puppies by tapping his fingers on the floor. Lee did this and Chrissy came over.

Brian and Lee lived in Herne Bay for six years, but the neighborhood was changing and they decided to move. They found a detached house that they liked with a patio and a large back garden for the dogs in Haslemere.

As Lee's German Shepherds began to age, they both developed serious health problems. The problems occurred first for Chrissy, who was older. She was unable to move her hind legs and could no longer walk. The vet could not do anything to help. She apparently was suffering from degenerative myelopathy. Fortunately, it is not a painful ailment. The vet suggested euthanasia, something to which Lee was vehemently opposed. To him, deliberately ending the life of his beloved dog was like ending the life of a family member just because that person could no longer walk. Indeed, for Lee, Chrissy was a family member. Lee kept Chrissy on a mat in his living room. He covered the mat with incontinence pads. They looked exactly like the ones Brian had used when Midnight became incontinent years earlier and reminded Brian of Midnight's last days. Lee turned Chrissy at least every four hours to prevent bedsores. He took care of his dog as one might care for a baby. She remained alert and appeared happy being with Lee.

When Chrissy died, Tiger was already experiencing severe health problems. He had a stroke and had lost the use of his hind legs. Again, the vet could only offer euthanasia, which Lee would not consider. Lee moved Tiger into his living room. He bought an air mattress to reduce bedsores and, as he did with Chrissy, he turned him at least every four hours. Also like Chrissy, Tiger remained alert and was clearly happy to be with Lee.

Brian and Lee's Relationship

Lee could have simply accepted Brian's financial support and remained idle, but that was not in Lee's character. He wanted to generate his own income as a property developer. To get him started, Brian helped him buy a rundown house at auction. Lee worked out a design for renovating the house that changed it from a three-bedroom house into a four-bedroom house. He taught himself how to do electrical work and plumbing and he became expert in all aspects of home renovations. With his partner George, he put enormous effort into renovating the house, moving walls and installing a new heating system. Lee liked to show Brian the things that he was now able to do and Brian was very impressed with his accomplishments. Although Brian had tried to steer Lee into an academic career, because that was what Brian was good at, he fully understood now that this was not what Lee wanted. Lee knew that he would be good at property development and he really is good at it.

The relationship between Brian and Lee had begun to change from client and escort to friends even from their first meeting. It was after less than a year that they made the change explicit. Lee stopped seeing clients and they agreed to end the escort and client relationship and to just see each other as friends. Brian enthusiastically welcomed this change. It was the relationship that he had always been looking for. Now a skeptic may wonder if Brian was just being naive and that "there's no fool like an old fool." No, their friendship was real.

Brian and Lee both were aware that others would not understand their relationship. After all, it was quite unusual. There are certainly well known instances of an older man marrying a younger woman, but Brian and Lee would not be married. And Brian and Lee were not partners. Lee has a partner with whom he has been even longer than he has known Brian. What then was Brian and Lee's relationship? They did not have a description that others would recognize. They jokingly referred to their relationship as "friends with benefits," alluding to a movie title, but their relationship was quite different from that of the couple in the movie who progressed from being friends to being lovers.

Some people might think that Lee was exploiting Brian. Brian had been giving Lee financial support for many years. He had bought a house for him and helped him start a business as a property developer. Brian had used almost all of his savings to buy and renovate the house for Lee and had mortgaged his own house to provide the funds for Lee's start in property development. Did Brian have to do these things to maintain his relationship with Lee? No, it was very clear to Brian that his relationship with Lee did not require those financial measures. Brian could have given Lee just enough financial support to allow him to give up escorting and that was indeed the arrangement for several years. But Brian's feelings for Lee were so deep that assuring a secure financial future for Lee was extremely important to Brian.

Lee worked hard fixing up the houses that they purchased, greatly increasing their sale value. His hard work and creativity allowed him to quickly move toward the secure future that Brian wanted for him. Brian was pleased with how Lee had increased the value of his properties. Brian now had less savings than when he met Lee and had a new mortgage on his home, but he had no regrets. Lee's success made him happier than anything that he could have purchased with that money. Lee has offered to pay off the mortgage that Brian took out on his own home to help Lee get started in property development. Brian told him that was not necessary. Brian knows that if he needs money for medical expenses or anything else he can count on Lee for it.

Some might think that Brian was exploiting Lee. When they met, Lee was a beautiful 18-year-old and Brian was an ordinary-looking 68-year-old. There was no question that Brian was deeply in love with Lee and no question that this love had a strong sexual component from the beginning. Brian knew that his physical attraction to Lee would not be reciprocated. He would have been very foolish to believe otherwise. Had Lee been a dishonest person he might have pretended to love Brian in the same way that Brian loved him, but Lee would not pretend this. So how did Lee feel about Brian? He told Brian that he loved him as a friend. That of course is an easy thing for someone to say. Was it really meaningful or was it just talk?

It is certainly not unusual for someone to love their best friend just as they would love a parent or a sibling. That love would not have a sexual component. Maybe we need to distinguish between being in love with someone and loving someone. You would not say that you were in love with a parent or sibling, but you would say that you loved them. It was clear to Lee that Brian was in love with him and clear to Brian that Lee was not in love with him, but Brian accepted the idea that Lee loved him as a friend. This asymmetry in their relationship could have been very awkward, but Lee handled it gracefully and Brian was pleased with the way Lee handled it.

Were Brian and Lee using each other? In an everyday sense of the word using, they were. Brian was getting what he wanted from Lee and Lee was getting what he wanted from Brian. There is another way to look at using, however. Lee had experiences with friends who had gotten what they wanted from him, such as his emotional support when they were troubled or the use of his renovation skills when they wanted to modify a kitchen or bathroom, and had shown little interest in maintaining a close friendship afterwards. This is what Lee saw as using. Certainly many of us have experienced that type of using.

Brian had similar experiences in his professional life. Twice the deans of his school had appointed him as an associate dean and made use of his administrative skills, but when he needed their support to rise to a higher position they did nothing to help. Brian and Lee recognized that their relationship is different from those relationships. There is complete honesty about what they want from each other and their friendship goes well beyond those things. Lee knows that Brian is not just using him to get what he wants and Brian knows that Lee is not just using him to get what he wants.

Brian and Lee consider each other to be best friends. Lee's relationships may seem unusual in that he has a partner and also a best friend. People often say that their spouse or partner is their best friend, so how could a partner and best friend be different people? This was indeed a problem early in Lee's relationship with Brian. George thought that Brian was trying to replace him as Lee's partner, but it became clear over time that this was not the case. How could George accept that Lee considers someone else to be his best friend? That could work only if Lee gives precedence to the status of partner over the status of best friend. As a corporate analogy, Brian was like a CEO but George was the chairman of the board.

Can people be regarded as best friends when they live more than 5000 miles apart and see each other only three times a year? If these visits were their only contact, then it would not be much of a friendship. You would want your best friend to be there when you had happy news to share and wanted to celebrate or you had sad news and wanted comfort and support. But these important aspects of friendship do not require in-person visits.

Brian remembers how he kept in touch with Harry forty years earlier. There were occasional letters and a few brief phone calls but it was not really possible to maintain a close friendship at that distance with the communications capabilities available at the time. Certainly there have been well-known friendships based on correspondence in past centuries, but this has become more difficult with the time constraints of modern living. Brian remembers that in the 1970s people described a future in which a person could go to a specially equipped office and place a video call to someone in another city. Of course there has been a giant leap in communications technology since the 1970s. Now you can place a video call to almost anywhere in the world as you walk down the street with your pocket size smart phone. Using apps such as Facetime or Skype you can talk as long as you like.

Brian had long been an early adopter of new technology and Lee is part of a generation that finds that technology to be a part of their daily lives. He likes to keep up with the latest in mobile phones. During the months when the two friends are more than 5000 miles apart there is a phone call, almost daily, that lasts from about an hour to as long as four hours. They also use technology that allows Brian and Lee to know what each other is doing from day to day or even minute to minute, regardless of their physical distance. They use the Find My Friends app to locate each other when they need to. For example, Brian does not want to phone or text Lee while Lee is driving, so he uses the app to make sure that Lee is not on the road before calling or texting. Brian gave Lee access to the six security cameras in his house so that Lee can check on his wellbeing. Brian has access to two cameras at Lee's house.

If Brian is deeply in love with Lee, why doesn't he move to

England so that he can see Lee more often? He wanted to move to England earlier in their relationship, but he had some issues to resolve first. His sister and her husband were getting on in years and he wanted to be close enough to visit them when necessary. He was getting on in years himself and Medicare would only cover medical expenses in the Unites States. Still, he was considering moving to England under a program called "Retired Person of Independent Means" for which he easily qualified. He finally decided to apply for this program in 2009. It was too late. The program had closed in 2008. He phoned a solicitor who specialized in immigration and asked why the program was closed. She told him that the government said they were not getting enough applications. This didn't make any sense to Brian. At the time they were admitting large numbers of people from some EU countries who couldn't support themselves and would be living on benefits when they moved to the U.K., but they would not admit an American who had a large retirement income and whose move to the U.K. would benefit their economy. What happened to the "special relationship" that was supposed to exist between the United States and the U.K.?

Even after being friends for more than fifteen years, Brian was still learning important new things about Lee. Brian had assumed that Lee would have been quite popular at school because he was so attractive. He thought he would have had lots of friends at school. He was quite surprised when Lee told him how things really were at his primary school. Popularity was not based on good looks and intelligence. It was based on wearing nice clothes and sneakers, on having a nice haircut and on playing sports. Lee's parents did not provide well for him. He wore shabby clothes and worn sneakers. He had incompetent haircuts done by his mother. He did not participate in sports. He didn't want to be one of the popular students. He wanted, perhaps unconsciously, to have the appearance of a nerd so that other students would not try to be his friends. He went as far as to deliberately do badly on vision tests so that he would be given glasses to wear. He was satisfied to be the least popular boy in his class.

Brian had similar experiences in elementary school and high school. Although his clothes were not shabby, they were typically out of style because his mother had no concept of what was considered stylish for a boy of his age. His father had no interest in sports and never taught him to play. His father made a belated attempt to do this after realizing that his son was considered backwards in sports, but this amounted to a few session of playing catch. He was the least popular boy in his class. He remembers occasions when the boys in the class were dividing into teams to play baseball. He was always the last to be chosen and the unlucky team members who had to choose him moaned loudly about it: "Oh no! Not Brian. We have to take Brian."

Brian and Lee's Travels

Brian and Lee made short trips outside of England almost every time Brian visited. They went to Spain, France, Monaco, Belgium, Denmark, Norway, the Netherlands, Germany, Italy and Ireland. Early in their relationship they made some trips by air and some by car. Lee developed a dislike of flying and preferred to travel by car. Brian liked to drive when he was younger, but now he really disliked travelling long distances by car. He found even a 90-minute drive to be unpleasant. He was still willing to travel by car on shorter trips, such as trips to Brussels or Paris. They especially enjoyed their visits to Brussels where they stayed at an apartment hotel. It was like a home away from home, with cooking, dishwashing and laundry facilities. They liked being able to shop at local markets and Lee was able to cook meals at their apartment. This gave their stay a cozy feeling.

Brian and Lee traveled to Berlin by air and spent a few days there. Brian was interested in seeing the remnants of the Berlin Wall. He remembers the troubling story from 1962 about a young man being shot by East German border guards while trying to cross from the Russian zone into the allied zones and left to bleed to death. There were many similar incidents and Brian saw these as horrible examples of man's inhumanity to man.

After walking along the wall they took a taxi back to their hotel. The driver was annoyed by the slow traffic and switched to another street. The other street was worse. The traffic was not moving at all. The driver exclaimed *Scheisse!* which is German for, "What have I done; this is much worse!"

A few years later Lee expressed an interest in visiting Berlin again. Because of his dislike of flying, he wanted to travel to Berlin by car. In addition to his general dislike of long car trips, Brian especially wanted to avoid travelling by car in Germany. Lee now drove a powerful car and on a previous trip to Germany he had enjoyed the stretches of the Autobahn that had no posted speed limit a little too much from Brian's viewpoint. Brian hated the road sign with the five diagonal stripes. He was nervous about high speed driving. Sometimes, without being aware of it, he would grip the edge of his seat. Lee would see this and say, "Why are you holding onto the seat? Do you think that the seat is going to save you?" Brian would let go of the seat, but when he became nervous again he gripped the seat again and everything was repeated. At Brian's insistence they made the trip by train. Lee went along with this although he didn't care much for train travel.

Lee particularly wanted to visit the C. Bechstein shop in Berlin. He had read that this shop not only had a large selection of high quality pianos but also featured exhibits of how pianos are constructed. Lee had a strong interest in pianos from childhood. They stayed at a hotel in central Berlin, a short walk from the Brandenburg gate. They took Uber to the Stilwerk Center and made their way to the top floor where they entered the C. Bechstein shop. The salesperson politely kept his distance and allowed them to look around freely. When Lee indicated that he was ready for assistance, the salesperson came over and began showing him around. Before long Lee and the salesperson were in a long discussion about the advantages and disadvantages of different types of pianos. Lee's knowledge of pianos clearly impressed the salesperson and Brian could only stand by and listen in awe as they talked. Lee knew what piano he wanted, but it was not something he would be able to afford in the near future so it became a goal toward which he would be working.

Brian and Lee travelled to Amsterdam in mid-December of 2016. Again it was difficult for them to agree on travel plans because of Lee's dislike of flying and Brian's dislike of long car journeys. The driving time from Calais to Amsterdam is 3 hours and 40 minutes. This is well beyond the amount of driving in one day with which Brian was comfortable.

There was another reason for not making the trip from Calais to Amsterdam and back to Calais by car. For some reason, French customs officers liked to harass British motorists returning home from France. Brian hated their rude questioning. They would ask about his relationship with Lee. "I'm in love with him and he loves me as a friend." No, Brian wouldn't give them that answer, even if they were French.

Lee was quite annoyed with the carelessness of the French officers in searching his car. He felt that they were damaging his car for no good reason. He insisted on watching them conduct their search, although they kept telling him to move away. One time they allowed a dog to go into the car without doing anything to protect the upholstery and that made Lee extremely angry. Brian and Lee never understood why the French were doing customs checks on vehicles traveling back to the U.K. when the British customs officers were just a few feet ahead. Shouldn't the French officers be checking vehicles entering France rather than vehicles leaving France? Brian was quite worried about Lee's angry reaction to the French searching his car. The French officers were armed and Brian feared that Lee could be arrested or worse.

Brian and Lee came up with a travel plan that assuaged both their concerns. They would take the ferry to Calais and drive to Antwerp, a distance that was tolerable for Brian. They would stay overnight in Antwerp and continue the trip to Amsterdam the next day. What about the dreaded French customs officers on their return trip? They would avoid them by returning directly by ferry from the Netherlands instead of returning by way of Calais.

On December 18 Lee and Brian travelled to Dover and entered the ferry port. There was a British immigration booth and a French immigration booth on the way to boarding the ferry. The British booth was unmanned. The agent in the French booth looked only at the covers of their British and American passports, not even opening them, and waved them through. There was never a problem with French immigration or customs when travelling to France, only when leaving France to return to England.

They drove directly from Calais to Antwerp and checked in at the Crowne Plaza, where they had stayed on a previous trip to Antwerp. They drove to the center of the city, parked and walked around. The Christmas decorations were up throughout the city center and this created a festive atmosphere. They found a nice Italian café and ordered pizza. The food was excellent and their whole experience in Antwerp was enjoyable. Although the reason for the stopover was that Brian did not like to travel long distances by car, they were glad that they had that evening in Antwerp.

The next morning Lee and Brian continued the trip to Amsterdam. They checked in at a Courtyard hotel on the outskirts of the city and later drove into the city center for dinner. Lee wanted to make a short trip to Aachen, Germany the next day. He was having a problem with his gearbox and on a previous trip to Germany he had his car worked on at Aachen and was impressed with that dealership. Brian knew that the trip to Aachen would involve travelling on the Autobahn and he decided to stay in Amsterdam and do some sightseeing instead. This was before he had to use a walker and he was accustomed to doing a lot of walking on his own.

Brian had read a novel that his sister recommended to him about Portuguese Jews who had migrated to Amsterdam in the seventeenth century. The Portuguese synagogue in that city was central to the story. Brian learned that this synagogue still existed and he wanted to see it. It was walking distance from the central train station.

As he got close to its location, he started looking at the GPS map on his phone to see if he was going in the right direction. A man who appeared to be in his early 60s came up to Brian and asked if he could help. Brian told him that he was looking for the Portuguese synagogue. The man pointed Brian in the right direction, and he did more than that. He told him some of the history of the Portuguese synagogue. Brian knew that Jews from Portugal and elsewhere in Europe had migrated to the Netherlands to escape persecution. What he didn't know was that the Dutch, while they allowed a synagogue to be constructed in central Amsterdam, required that it be back from the street. To accomplish this the people who arranged for it to be built put small houses all around the actual synagogue. Brian went there and could see the small houses that surrounded the synagogue building. He found this visible piece of history intriguing. He was grateful to the man who told him about this. The kind advice of a helpful local can be of great value to a tourist. Although Brian had not attended religious services as an adult, he remembered the traditional layout of a synagogue from his childhood and was fascinated seeing the same layout in a synagogue that was hundreds of years old.

Brian and Lee arranged to meet at a Chinese restaurant in central Amsterdam that evening when Lee returned from Germany. It was a bit crowded but the food was excellent and they enjoyed the meal. They had wanted to visit the Anne Frank House, but it was already too late to reserve a time slot for the visit when they made their travel plans.

The return trip began with a drive from Amsterdam to the ferry port at Hook van Holland. Brian and Lee were passed though by

Dutch and British customs and immigration with no damaging searches and no awkward relationship questions. They had booked a Captain's Class 2-berth window cabin, which was quite comfortable and cozy. Although the trip was longer than the trip would have been by way of Calais, avoiding the French customs and immigration people was worth it. The ferry arrived at Harwich and they had to drive to Haslemere. Brian wanted to avoid the Dartford Crossing because the southbound route went over the QE2 Bridge and Brian found crossing that high bridge extremely stressful. They did not find an alternate route, however, and Brian asked Lee to warn him before the bridge became visible. Brian closed his eyes and kept them closed until they were over the bridge.

During another of Brian's visits to Lee's home they decided to travel to Dublin, rather than travel to somewhere on the continent. One reason for this choice was similar to the reason they returned from Amsterdam directly from the Netherlands instead of going through France. It was their disdain for the way the French officials handled departing visitors. Those practices likely harmed the French economy by discouraging tourism and their choice of going to Ireland rather than to continental Europe was an example of that.

They planned to drive from London to Holyhead and to take the ferry to Dublin. They made one mistake in setting the navigator in Lee's car. They selected the option of taking the shortest route to Holyhead. The shortest route, however, went over a mountain. It was not a very high mountain but it was high enough for acrophobic Brian to be terrified. He kept asking Lee to drive slower but Lee couldn't because there was traffic behind them and no way for other cars to pass. Brian was relieved when they finally came out of the mountain and arrived at the approach to the ferry port.

The ferry trip to Dublin was uneventful and they stayed at a hotel north of the city. The next day they drove to Newgrange, a 5000-year-old passage tomb that is largely intact. They walked through a narrow passage that led to the central chamber. The guide explained that the passage was designed to be illuminated at the winter solstice. Visiting Newgrange was like traveling to a different world, a world that existed 5000 years ago.

Brian's Vertigo

Brian remained in good health throughout his 60s. Several times a week he took a brisk 3-mile walk, stopping for frozen yogurt on the way. Shortly after turning 70 he suffered a sudden and severe vertigo episode. He felt the room spinning rapidly in all directions. This was very frightening, as anyone who has experienced severe vertigo could tell you. It was completely disabling. He stayed in bed for about an hour with his eyes closed, but the vertigo did not subside. He called 911 and they sent an ambulance. The operator asked if he could open a door for the paramedics. He managed with some difficulty to crawl to the nearest door, a side-door opening into the bathroom adjacent to the master bedroom. The operator stayed on the line until he got back onto his bed.

The paramedics arrived quickly and asked Brian if he could walk to the ambulance outside the front door. He said that he could not so they brought in a gurney and moved him onto it. He opened his eyes briefly in the ambulance on the way to the hospital. The world was still spinning. An MRI was taken of his brain. They did not find a cause for the vertigo. He was given meclizine and a scopolamine patch to wear behind his ear. By morning the vertigo had subsided and he was released from the hospital. After that incident Brian kept over-the-counter meclizine tablets in his house in case the vertigo symptoms should recur. He also replaced the lock on his front door with a combination lock and gave the combination to the fire department in case it became necessary again to call for paramedics.

About seven years later another vertigo attack occurred and neither of the two precautions that Brian had taken was effective. Brian kept the meclizine in a kitchen cupboard, but he could not get to the kitchen because of the vertigo. He waited in bed for a few hours, hoping that the vertigo would subside, but it did not and he called 911. The paramedics came to the front door, but they were unable to open it. They apparently believed that the lock would be released once they entered the combination. That was not the case. You have to enter the combination and then turn a knob to release the lock. With great difficulty, Brian crawled to the front door and opened it. Because he was already at the front door, the paramedics helped him outside and got him into to the ambulance in his driveway. At the hospital they did not do a brain scan this time. That may have been because a stroke was not regarded as a likely cause of vertigo or because of the time that had passed since the vertigo began, suggesting that it was too late for an effective stroke treatment.

Brian was admitted to the hospital and stayed there overnight. The vertigo did not clear up as quickly as it had the previous time. The doctor did not use a scopolamine patch because of concern about side effects in older patients. The next morning the doctor asked Brian whether he lived alone. When he said that he did, the doctor told him that he was not stable enough to be at home alone and presented two options. The first was to be moved to an extended care facility, that is, a nursing home. The second was to have a care person take him home and stay until he was sufficiently recovered to be on his own. Brian did not like the idea of entering a nursing home, so he went with the second option. He was given a list of senior care agencies and he selected one. He was pleased with the care that he received. The carer arrived at the hospital within an hour. Brian wanted to go to the bathroom just before that and the nurse said that was not stable enough and would have to use a bedpan. Brian refused. When the carer from the agency arrived, he told her that he wanted assistance in getting to the bathroom and she did that for him.

When Brian was ready to leave the hospital, the carer took him in a wheelchair, as required by the hospital, to her car that she had managed to park close to the hospital door. The hospital provided him with a walker to take home. The carer assisted him through the rest of the day and part of the next day until he felt stable enough to be on his own. He was pleased with the carer and he decided to use that agency if he needed home care again.

Brian stayed in bed at home for the next day. By evening he was able to move around the house using the walker and the carer was not needed overnight. The next day the carer returned and helped with shopping and meal preparation as the vertigo continued to subside. Brian was able to drive after a few days and could do his own grocery shopping, but some dizziness persisted for several weeks. His walking was unsteady and he had some pain in his hip area while walking.

The vertigo episode raised concerns with Lee about Brian living alone safely. Brian gave Lee the phone number of the local fire department for emergencies. One day Brian went out to do some grocery shopping and forgot to take his cell phone. When he returned home there was a fire truck in his driveway. The people from the fire department told him that they had received a request by phone for a welfare check. They said that they were glad that he was fine and they were very nice about it. Brian's neighbors were standing outside and Brian told them that a concerned friend had phoned the fire department. One neighbor said to Brian, "You must have a very good friend."

Lee told Brian that he had called the paramedics because he was unable to reach him on the phone. He couldn't see him on a camera and he was afraid that something had happened to him.

Over the next year Brian saw an otologist about his balance difficulties and an orthopedist about his hip pain. He also began physical therapy. He had difficulty staying balanced while walking and he began to use a cane. Soon the pain prevented him from walking even short distances. Lee suggested that he use a four-wheel walker or rollator, but he wanted to manage with just a cane. Eventually he did purchase a rollator and he was able to walk outdoors again without pain. The physical therapist was in support of his using of a rollator. Both the otologist and the orthopedist recommended that he see a neurologist about the dizziness. He was hesitant about this and waited almost a year. He finally consulted a neurologist who ordered a brain MRI.

Brian's primary care physician received a copy of the MRI and phoned Brian with the results about a week before his next appointment with the neurologist. His primary care physician told him that the MRI showed enlarged ventricles and that he thought the neurologist might tell him that he had normal pressure hydrocephalus (NPH). Brian researched this and found that indeed people suffering from NPH had difficulty walking as did Brian and he became convinced that he did have NPH.

The treatment that he found in researching NPH was drilling a hole in the skull and running a tube into the abdomen to drain the excess fluid. Brian was terrified. He went to his next appointment with the neurologist expecting an NPH diagnosis and thinking that the neurologist would order a spinal tap to confirm the diagnosis.

He asked the neurologist if the MRI indicated that he had NPH, expecting a positive answer.

The neurologist told him that the MRI did not indicate NPH and that his walking problem was not the same as the gait problem found with NPH. The neurologist said that the MRI indicated that he had had mini strokes. He was extremely relieved to learn that he did not have NPH. Probably no one had ever been so happy to hear that he had had strokes. Brian joked with Lee that he needed an NPH diagnosis like a hole in the head. The neurologist prescribed a statin and a blood thinning medicine to help prevent future strokes.

Having been through two severe vertigo episodes, Brian was fearful that it would happen again. He remembered the two episodes as the worst things that he had ever experienced. Each of the previous episodes required a call to 911, a ride to the hospital in an ambulance and an overnight stay at the hospital. Brian prepared for the possibility of another vertigo episode in the hope that he could avoid the ambulance and the hospital. He started to carry chewable meclizine tablets at all times and he kept some on a table next to his bed. He also kept a phone, the phone number of the senior care agency that he had used and a urinal within reach of his bed, knowing that he might not be able to get out of bed on his own during a vertigo episode. Early one morning he got out of bed briefly and went back to bed. It was either when he put his head down on the pillow or when he started to lift his head again that the room appeared to be in rapid motion. It was another vertigo attack.

This time he decided not to call 911. He called the senior care agency and requested that they send someone to stay with him. They said that would take a couple of hours and in the meantime they sent an administrative person. Someone showed up with paperwork in about an hour. They wanted a credit card and Brian told them where to find his wallet. He thought that he may have signed something, but he was not able to read anything with the nystagmus that he was experiencing.

The carer showed up about an hour later. She tried to be helpful but her communication skills were not very good and she had difficulty understanding what Brian asked her to do. Still the help that she provided was adequate. Brian needed help to get from his bed into the bathroom and to get back to bed.

Brian thought about phoning Lee, but he knew that Lee would

want to fly to California immediately when he heard about Brian's situation. He decided to wait for a few hours to see if his condition improved. Although he had a walker, he was not able to walk even a few feet to the bathroom safely and he needed someone to be there to keep him from falling. He felt nauseous all day and could only eat some yogurt.

Brian phoned Lee that afternoon, which was nighttime in England, and as expected Lee wanted to fly to California immediately. It was too late to get a flight that night and Lee started looking into flights for the next day. Although Brian knew that the past vertigo episodes each lasted for only a few days, he could not be sure of what would happen this time and he gave Lee a mixed message about traveling. He liked the idea of Lee visiting and replacing the carers provided by the agency. Lee would have provided Brian both the practical help and the emotional support that he needed to get through the vertigo episode. It would have been the difference between being helped by someone who was like family to Brian and someone just paid an hourly wage to provide some help.

Brian did not discourage Lee from making the long trip, but at the same time he told him to wait a little longer before committing to travel. The next morning Brian was still experiencing vertigo, perhaps somewhat less severe. During the two previous vertigo episodes he had experienced rotation about multiple axes, which made the episodes completely incapacitating. The current episode was like that at the beginning, but later the motion was limited to rotation about a vertical axis.

Brian knew about two things that he could try. After one of the previous episodes his otologist told him to move his eye in the direction opposite the direction of the perceived motion. This was difficult because the direction of the perceived motion would change and sometimes the motion was too rapid. He had little success with that method. The other method, which was based on his knowledge of perception and also was suggested by a nurse at the end of his previous hospital stay for vertigo, was to fixate a spot on the wall. He did this, trying his best to will the spot to remain stationary and it worked some of the time. It felt to him as if he were applying a brake to the moving scene. He told the neurologist about it and the neurologist said, "I'm surprised that you have a spot on your wall."

In the meantime, Lee had actually purchased a ticket to leave for Los Angeles the next day. There was an unforeseen problem, however. Lee did not have a current ETSA, which is required for travel to the United States from a visa-waiver country. He had not been told by the airline about this requirement when he booked his ticket, but when he tried to check in online he was told that he must have an ETSA. He looked into this and found that it could take up to 72 hours to get one, but his flight was leaving in less than 24 hours. He phoned the airline and they told him that he could take a later flight after paying a change fee. They failed to tell him that he could cancel the flight without charge because it was less than 24 hours since he had ticketed. When he phoned the airline again, demanding that they cancel the ticket and refund the full amount because they failed to tell him that he needed an ETSA when he booked, they agreed to this because it was in keeping with their policy of refunding tickets for flights that were cancelled within 24 hours. He was pleased that they would provide a full refund but annoyed at being misled by the airline agent the first time he phoned. Lee immediately applied for an ETSA and has been keeping it up to date in case he should need to go to California on short notice.

At the same time, Brian was recovering from the vertigo episode and he told Lee that there was no need for him to make the trip. All in all Brian had care provided by the agency for the first day of the episode, overnight care that night, care the second day, overnight care that night and care for part of the third day with no overnight care. He was able to manage on his own after that. He did not drive for another week but used Whole Food's delivery service during that period.

Brian's Prostate Cancer

Brian had been undergoing annual physical exams for more than ten years and they had always shown him to be in excellent health. At times his LDL cholesterol level was too high and on one occasion his doctor gave him a prescription for a statin, telling him he could try to bring the level down before filling the prescription. Brian began attending to his diet more closely, eliminating red meat and eating oat bran for breakfast. This successfully lowered his LDL level and he did not fill the statin prescription at that time. As Brian grew older, his PSA level began to rise. His doctor referred him to a urologist who wanted to do a biopsy of the prostate. Brian researched this and decided that he would like to have an ultrasound before deciding on a biopsy. He asked the urologist if he could have a color doppler ultrasound. The urologist asked Brian if he was an engineer. Brian was not happy about that question. It indicated to him that the urologist did not appreciate patients who did their own research about diagnostic methods and treatments.

The urologist recommended combining an ultrasound with a biopsy, but Brian insisted on an ultrasound only. The ultrasound results were negative and Brian decided not to do a biopsy without imagery showing specifically where the biopsy should be taken. He had read about people being subjected to multiple biopsies without any positive findings of prostate cancer.

Brian read about a new test for prostate cancer that had not yet been approved in the United States, but was in use in the United Kingdom. He arranged to have this test done at a prostate clinic in London on his next visit. The test results were negative, but the British urologist suggested that an MRI would be more definitive. The American urologist had not recommended an MRI and Medicare did not pay for that test at the time, only for ultrasound. Brian's PSA level was now rising rapidly and his American primary care physician strongly advised him to have a biopsy.

On a subsequent visit to England, Brian made an appointment for an MRI at the same British prostate clinic. He wanted the biopsy to be guided by imagery showing any suspect areas. It was to be a contrast MRI and he was told that he would need to have a blood test for kidney function first.

Lee drove Brian to an NHS hospital in Canterbury for the blood test. The day before the scheduled MRI Brian learned that the hospital would not fax the results of the blood test to the London clinic as he had expected. Lee quickly drove him back to the hospital where they agreed to give him the results in a sealed envelope. It was just a plain envelope. Brian wanted to verify that the envelope contained the necessary test results so he opened it after leaving the hospital. He inspected the document and put it in another plain envelope, which he sealed and addressed to the London clinic.

The next day Lee drove Brian from his home in Herne Bay to the MRI facility in London. As Brian was preparing to change into a hospital gown, a technician came into the dressing room and told him they could not do the MRI that day. Brian was shocked, but the technician went on to explain that they had not yet received the required blood test results. Brian happily took the envelope, which he himself had sealed and on which he had written the name of the clinic, out of his pocket. He handed it to the technician. The technician opened it, looked at the lab results and said that they could now proceed with the MRI. Brian had no problem with the MRI. Lee picked him up at the clinic afterwards and they returned to Herne Bay.

Brian had an appointment with the British urologist a few days later to review the MRI results and Lee once again drove him to London. The urologist showed Brian the MRI images and pointed out spots that were suspect. He strongly urged Brian to have those spots biopsied and recommended a radiologist who he said was the best in England. Brian made an appointment for the biopsy the next week.

The evening before the biopsy appointment, Brian and Lee discussed when they would need to leave for London the next morning. Brian was concerned about being late and losing the appointment slot and he wanted to leave two hours before the scheduled appointment, but Lee, who would be driving, said it shouldn't take that long and that they could leave just over an hour ahead of the appointment. In the morning Brian woke Lee about two hours before the appointment time. Lee said it was too early and refused to get ready to leave. Brian, who tends to be overly cautious about such things, knew that he would have to leave immediately if he were to go to London by bus and train. When Lee continued to refuse to leave right away, Brian left and took a bus to the nearby train station where he could get a local train to the Canterbury station and change to a London-bound high-speed train. While he waited for the local train he saw Lee walking towards him from across the street.

"What are you doing?" Lee said, sounding quite annoyed. "I was going to drive you to London."

Still concerned about being late, Brian replied, "You said you wouldn't leave right away so I thought I had better take the train."

"Well I'll drive you there now."

"I can take the train. You can pick me up at the clinic after the biopsy."

"No, I'll drive you there and back. But I have to go back home and get ready and you've just lost time by trying to take the train."

Lee's car was across the street. Brian went back to Lee's house with him. Lee got ready and they headed for London. Brian was quite upset. He was not only worried about being late for the biopsy appointment but he thought that Lee was angry with him for leaving on his own and trying to take the train. He felt that he had made a foolish mistake thinking that Lee wouldn't take him to London in time for his appointment.

Around 10 minutes later, as they were driving toward London, Lee said something that caused Brian to begin to cry: "I'm sorry about earlier. I had just gotten up. I didn't really mean that I wouldn't take you to London right away."

Lee asked Brian why he was crying, but Brian couldn't tell him, although he did explain it years later. Brian tended to cry when an emotional burden was removed. Brian thought that his best friend, whose support he really needed at the time, was angry with him for trying to take the train. When Lee said that he was sorry about saying that he would not leave for London right away, Brian realized that Lee was not angry with him and was taking responsibility for the misunderstanding earlier. It was the feeling of relief that his friend was not angry with him that caused Brian to cry as they drove toward London.

There was heavy traffic entering London and with the time lost because of Brian going to the train station they just made it to the clinic in time for Brian's appointment. Lee waited in the reception room and Brian was taken into the examination room. The radiologist viewed a display of the MRI superimposed on a real-time ultrasound showing the location of his probe. This was exactly how Brian understood that a biopsy should be done. Because Brian had scar tissue from two previous hemorrhoid surgeries, the insertion of the probe was extremely painful. Once the probe was inserted, the collection of the samples was not painful.

The procedure was soon completed and Brian was taken to a recovery room. He was feeling light-headed after the procedure. The clinic staff was very kind and helpful. They brought Lee to the recovery room and brought both of them cups of hot chocolate. In that moment Brian understood even more the value of having a friend like Lee. Lee not only drove Brian to London for the biopsy appointment but, more importantly, he provided the emotional support that helped Brian deal with that procedure.

Lee stayed with Brian in the recovery room until Brian felt stable enough to leave the clinic. He took Brian's arm as they left, to make sure that he would not fall after his difficult experience undergoing the biopsy. They walked a short distance to the John Lewis store in Oxford Street and went to the cafeteria. It was close to Christmas and the cafeteria was serving a special turkey dinner with trimmings. They enjoyed the meal and Brian still has pleasant memories of that afternoon. The enjoyable dinner with Lee more than made up for the difficult time at the clinic.

Brian made an appointment with the urologist three days later to get the results of the biopsy. They drove into London again and Lee waited for Brian in the clinic's reception room while he met with the urologist. The urologist first asked Brian if Lee was his son and Brian explained that he was a friend. Brian only half-understood that this question meant that he was about to get some bad news. The urologist went on to tell Brian that he had prostate cancer and that it was of a type that needed to be treated as soon as possible. He discussed possible treatments, specifically surgery and radiation.

Brian told the urologist that he would have the treatments after returning home in about a week. The British urologist looked through a list of urologists in Southern California. He came across what appeared to be a Jewish last name and suggested to Brian, who has a clearly Jewish last name, that he might prefer that urologist. He made an indirect reference to the match in ethnicity. Brian was shocked by what he considered to be an anti-Semitic comment, but he was otherwise very pleased with the urologist and was willing to believe that the comment was made out of ignorance and that the urologist meant no offense. He did not say anything, but the urologist likely picked up his shocked expression and did not make that type of suggestion again.

The urologist gave Brian a handful of brochures dealing with prostate cancer and the consultation was over. Brian joined Lee in the reception room and told him about the diagnosis as they left the clinic, although Lee would have already understood what the diagnosis was from the stack of prostate cancer brochures that Brian was carrying. Indeed, Lee was annoyed that the clinic staff had not put the brochures in an envelope, feeling that leaving Brian to carry them loose out of the clinic was invading his privacy. Brian did not show much of a reaction to the bad news. He saw it as a new problem that he would have to face and he knew that he could deal with the problem with Lee's support.

Brian and Lee went to John Lewis for their special turkey dinner once again. When they finished dinner it was in the peak traffic hour, so they decided to stay in London a bit longer. They walked around on Oxford Street, looking at shop windows, visiting a large toy store and reading the posters outside the wax museum. Then they returned to the John Lewis cafeteria for some desert. After that they went to Lee's car, which was in an underground car park near the John Lewis store, and drove back to Herne Bay. Brian has happy memories of that late afternoon in London even though it began with a cancer diagnosis.

The day after Brian received the prostate cancer diagnosis he phoned his primary care physician in California. He wanted an appointment with a urologist, other than the one he had been seeing previously in California, who would manage his treatment. It was between Christmas and New Year's and it was difficult to get an appointment, but his primary care physician arranged an appointment for him with a urologist the first week in January. Brian looked up the urologist and learned that he specialized in robotic surgery for removing the prostate. Brian didn't want surgery and he was hesitant about seeing that urologist, but he went ahead with his appointment.

When he told the urologist that he had already been diagnosed with prostate cancer, the urologist, whose schedule was quite full, had him return for a second appointment the same day after his normal office hours. This was because the urologist wanted to spend more time with him so that he could fully discuss treatment options. To Brian's relief, the urologist did not push surgery. He listened to what Brian wanted and commented positively about Brian's insistence on having an MRI before agreeing to a biopsy. Brian wanted his prostate cancer to be treated with radiation. He was very pleased with this urologist. After the inappropriate remark by the British urologist, he noted that the American urologist that he had stopped seeing previously had a clearly Jewish surname and the urologist that he now preferred had a name that indicated Japanese ancestry. Ethnicity was completely irrelevant to Brian's choice of a urologist to see him through the prostate cancer treatment.

The urologist told Brian that radiation could be accompanied by a hormonal treatment to make the prostate nonfunctional, at least temporarily. The urologist referred Brian to a radiologist who specialized in cancer treatment and was the senior radiologist at the main hospital in Brian's area.

Brian saw the radiologist on a Friday afternoon. He remembers that because he had the weekend to make an important decision about the treatment. The radiologist talked with him at length about the options that the urologist had described: The radiation treatment could or could not be accompanied by hormonal treatment to shut down the prostate. The radiologist did not make a recommendation, but left it to Brian to make the decision. He indicated that Brian should give him his decision by Monday morning so as not to delay treatment.

This was a difficult decision. Research on the hormonal treatment indicated that the cancer was less likely to recur if that treatment accompanied radiation, but the hormonal treatment had unpleasant side effects. Brian was undecided. He vacillated between wanting to include the hormonal treatment and wanting to reject it. He needed to talk about it and he spoke with Lee several times during the weekend. Lee did not try to influence his decision,

115

but helped Brian make his own choice. Brian downloaded an article from a medical journal that was purported to support use of the hormonal treatment. He learned that the recommendation of that treatment was based on a retrospective study and that clinical trials were planned, but had not yet taken place. Brian decided to reject the hormonal treatment and Lee was supportive of his decision.

The radiation treatment took place at a hospital near Brian's home, five days a week for two months. The procedure was to check in at the reception desk, go to a dressing room, remove everything below the waist and change into a hospital gown. It was one of those typical ridiculous gowns that left your butt exposed unless you were extremely skilled at tying bows behind your back. There was even a cartoon in the dressing room showing a patient wearing a hospital gown with his butt exposed and someone saying, "Now I know why they call it ICU."

Although the treatment was not at all painful, Brian found it unpleasant for two reasons. Brian is not a very sociable person and he was uncomfortable about seeing receptionists, technicians, nurses and other patients every weekday. This was years after he had retired from his position as a university professor and he was not used to dealing with people on a daily basis. Worse than that was the requirement that he drink 24 ounces of water before each treatment and not empty his bladder until after the treatment. He found that extremely uncomfortable. He knew that this was necessary to move his bladder away from his prostate to avoid damage to the bladder and he learned later that this precaution by the radiologist was successful. It was a daily phone conversation with Lee that helped Brian get through those two months of unpleasant treatment sessions. The radiation therapy was successful and the urologist seemed pleasantly surprised that Brian's PSA readings had dropped to a low level without the hormonal treatment.

Lee's Maternal Grandmother

Lee's maternal grandmother played an essential role in his life when he was a child and this continued into his adult life. She came across as being a strict and formidable person, but in reality she was an emotional person with a big heart. People took advantage of her kindness and this caused her to develop a hard shell for her own protection, much like Lee had been forced to develop when he was unfairly expelled from Mansea Hall. Lee and his nan really understood each other and their relationship remained very close to the end of her life.

Even after he moved to Kent and later to Surrey, Lee visited his nan in London frequently. Her children and her other grandchildren were of little help to her as she grew older. Her youngest daughter claimed to be helping her and was receiving an allowance from Social Services, but she did almost nothing for her mum. Instead, she was just helping herself to her mum's money. She would use her mum's bankcard to withdraw cash, supposedly to buy groceries for her mum, but the cash that she withdrew exceeded what she actually spent on groceries. Of his nan's children and grandchildren, only Lee made a serious effort to help her as she grew older. When he visited her he would often clean her entire flat. He would repair appliances or, if they could not be repaired, he would help her order replacements. He told his nan that her youngest daughter was taking advantage of her and although his nan believed him, she didn't want to confront her daughter. She was afraid that might end their relationship and she would rather have a relationship in which her daughter was using her than no relationship at all.

Lee's nan had been having a number of medical problems. She had two hip replacement surgeries and was having difficulty getting around. She had been complaining about back pain and an NHS physician was having her take a prescription pain medicine. She had lumps on her skin and the physician said that they were cysts and told her to use an over-the-counter skin cream. Before Lee's last visit to her flat she had become increasingly ill and was not eating. She complained about difficulty breathing and continuing pain. An NHS physician came to her flat and checked her oxygen saturation level. He said that it was in the acceptable range and he told her to take paracetamol for the pain, making no attempt to determine the underlying cause of her pain.

When Lee visited his nan the next day he found her confused and unable to eat or drink. He called 999 and requested an ambulance. Although he told them that she was having severe difficulty breathing, they told him that because she was sitting up and talking her condition did not constitute an emergency. They refused to send an ambulance. After repeated calls over a five-hour period, they finally sent a van that took her to a nearby hospital.

The physician at the hospital at first refused to admit her. Once again she was told that her condition did not constitute an emergency. Only after insistence by Lee, Lee's mum and another of his nan's daughters, the physician agreed to order an X-ray. The X-ray revealed that she was suffering from pneumonia. They also found an irregular heartbeat. The physician discovered lumps throughout her body and said that a CT scan was necessary. Despite the physician's indication that a scan was necessary, and repeated requests by Lee and his nan's daughters that it be performed, no scan was performed. It was only after Lee said that he would take her to a private hospital for a scan that a scan was finally scheduled two weeks later. The scan showed cancer throughout her body and the physician told them that it was terminal.

Lee's nan was placed in a four-bed ward on the top floor in an area set aside exclusively for elderly patients. She strongly indicated a wish to go home and Lee and her daughters requested that she receive care at home, including hospice care if appropriate, but nothing was done about this. A consultant confirmed that she had cancer all over her body and said that anything could happen, but that she could have months to live. It was March 2016 and the consultant gave the family false hope by saying that they should make her Christmas a special one and that she did not qualify for hospice care.

Lee's nan was treated poorly at the hospital. She was screaming in pain when they changed her diaper, but she did not complain about the rough handling, instead apologizing for screaming and thanking the nurse. Lee visited his nan at the hospital every day for the next three weeks. During that time no one asked if she had dentures and her dentures were never cleaned. It was only when she was dying and Lee asked the nurse about dentures that the nurse realized that she had them.

Lee noticed while visiting his nan that other patients were being treated poorly as well. One patient in the ward was forced to sit in a chair although she wanted desperately to go back to bed. Yes, there may have been medical reasons for having a patient sit in a chair for four hours a day, but that patient could not tolerate it and her pain and discomfort was ignored. Another patient found that she was unable to call for help because she could not reach the button for her buzzer. Lee helped her find the button, which had been tucked under her mattress and disconnected. He reconnected it and she used it to call for help. It was obvious from the nurse's reaction that it had been disconnected and hidden deliberately so that the nurses wouldn't be bothered. Lee also observed that another patient had dentures that were not taken out and cleaned at night.

Lee did not like seeing people being disrespected, especially elderly people. He observed a nurse dealing with an older woman who had become disoriented, probably from the medication that she had been receiving. The woman said to the nurse, "What are you doing in my kitchen? Get out of my kitchen."

The nurse replied, "You are not in your kitchen. You are in hospital."

The nurse laughed and looked at Lee, probably expecting him to laugh as well. Lee didn't think that was funny. He thought that there was no need for the nurse to upset the woman that way. The nurse mocked the woman, imitating her saying, "Get out of my kitchen."

The nurse left and the woman asked Lee, "Do you like my kitchen?" Lee replied, "It's a nice kitchen."

Then she asked, "Do you like my sink?"

Lee replied, "It's a very nice sink."

The woman told Lee that her phone had been ringing and she wasn't able to reach it. Lee found her phone. The nurse had moved it out of reach. She had missed calls from her daughter. She tried to call her daughter, but her credit had run out. Lee found her daughter's number under missed calls on the woman's phone and placed a call to her daughter on his own phone. He explained to her daughter that he was someone visiting at the hospital and he handed the phone to the woman. The woman was so happy to get to talk to her daughter that she began to cry. She could not stop thanking Lee afterwards. Her daughter later came to visit.

Lee's nan also was confused at times, probably also from the medication. She thought that her sheet was a dressing gown. She asked Lee if he liked her dressing gown and he said that it looked warm and cozy.

Lee was worried about his nan's condition and although he tried not to show it when he visited her at the hospital, one day she noticed this and it upset her. She said to Lee, "Why do you come here and look so miserable?"

Lee said, "I'm going then," and started to walk to the door.

His nan said, "Oh, no Lee. Don't go."

Lee will never forget the pain in her voice when she thought that he was leaving. She really needed him to stay. It was like the pain that Brian heard in Lee's voice early in their relationship when he thought that Brian had abandoned him at a hotel. Lee's nan changed completely from being aggressive to being vulnerable and nice. Lee knew that she was thinking that he was really leaving and this made him sad. He went right back to her bedside and said, "I'm not going. I'm just getting a drink."

Lee's nan wanted very much to go home, but Social Services took more than a week to process her request and by then she was too ill to go home. Yet the medical staff seemed to want her to go home and decided not to put her on intravenous fluids although she was not drinking and it was clear even to her family that she was seriously dehydrated. Lee told the medical staff that his nan was not eating and drinking, but they looked at the nurses' entries and told him that she was eating and drinking. Yet at least one member of her family was with her at all times and they knew that the nurses' entries were not accurate.

Lee's nan had a comfortable chair at first, but this was taken away and given to another patient. Instead she was put in a flimsy chair and left unattended. She fell from the chair and hit her head. There was blood on her tongue. Her condition went downhill from that point and she was moved to a side room. It was the hospital's practice to move a patient who was dying to one of those private rooms.

The level of care continued to be poor. The nurses failed to keep Lee's nan's mouth moist and it became dry and started bleeding. Lee was told that he would be provided with a spray for her mouth and that a nurse from hospice care would show him how to use it, but by the time they provided the spray her mouth was bleeding with blood running into her throat, causing a cackle. Lee tried to keep her mouth moist with water. A few times when she felt someone wetting her mouth with a sponge, she looked angry at first, but when she saw that it was Lee she smiled.

Lee and his nan's daughters could plainly see that she was near death, yet the medical staff told them that she could have many months to live. The failure of the medical staff to recognize the gravity of her condition and their use of inaccurate entries from the nurses to evaluate her condition led to extremely troubling consequences. First, the requests that she be given hospice care, which might have led to a more dignified and peaceful end of life, were denied. Second, her family could have had many more hours with her near the end of her life if her condition had been accurately reported to them.

One day when Lee, Lee's mum and another of his nan's daughters were in the room, his nan kept calling his name. The other daughter, not Lee's mom, was envious of his nan's affection for Lee and actually said to her, "Call my name."

Although Lee's nan had been disoriented at times during her stay at the hospital, she became exactly herself just before she died. There was no confusion. She said, "I'm dead now; this is it." Lee began to cry. His nan saw this and panicked a bit. She knew it was really the end.

Lee said, "You're not dead."

She said, "I'm trying not to be dead."

He said, "I know this is scary. This is something we all have to go through and you're very brave."

The last time his nan was conscious she looked at Lee and smiled. It was a smile that showed a lot of love and affection. Lee's mum remembers this as well.

Two of the nurses caring for Lee's nan were genuinely kindhearted people. One was a student nurse who liked his nan and thought she could be funny at times. Lee spoke with her a couple of times. She shared his feeling that older people should be treated with love and respect. She shared his understanding that these people are the grandparents, older friends and teachers who were there for us when we were young and they should not be separated or treated in a different way because they have grown older. She was there just after Lee's nan died and Lee told her that her feeling about how older people should be treated would make her a very good nurse. Lee saying something nice to her, just after losing his beloved nan, touched her and she began to cry.

Another nurse had noticed that Lee was by his nan's bedside day and night for weeks. She understood how much Lee loved his nan and she couldn't talk to Lee because it would be too painful.

Lee is troubled by the thought that his nan could still be with us if the NHS GP had properly investigated the causes of her pains and lumps. Their refusal to send an ambulance when requested, their delay in performing an X-ray and a CT scan and her poor treatment at the hospital also may have hastened her death. Equally troubling was their use of incorrect observations by the nurses that failed to show that she had stopped eating and drinking, to deny her hospice care. They denied his nan a peaceful and dignified death surrounded by her family and denied her family the time to say goodbye.

Brian was scheduled to visit Lee while Lee's nan was in the hospital. He decided to go ahead with the trip, even knowing that Lee would be visiting at the hospital most of the time. He had a key to Lee's house and he knew how to get there from the airport by public transportation. A few days later, Lee came home late at night. Brian had never before seen Lee so upset. He knew immediately what had happened. His nan had died. Lee was at the hospital for her final moments. Although she was heavily drugged and was not always aware of her surroundings, she knew that Lee was there and she said goodbye in her own way.

Lee to this day regrets not having defied the hospital staff and taken his nan home, but of course that would not have been possible. He was not her next of kin. Her children were making the decisions and as a grandchild he had no say in this. Lee had done everything he could have for his nan, but he had no legal basis for making decisions about her care. That made Brian think about what would happen if he became ill and couldn't care for himself. Brian knew that his sister could be trusted to make important decisions, but she was older and had health problems of her own. With the exception of his sister, the only person Brian trusted to make decisions about his health was Lee.

After seeing how Lee had cared for his nan despite the obstacles placed in his path by his not having legal authority to manage her care, Brian decided to give Lee legal authority to make both health and financial decisions for him should he be unable to do so himself. When he returned to California he worked with a lawyer to do this. As Brian reviewed the draft documents, he noticed a provision that if the appointed health care agent, who would be Lee, and the doctors disagreed, the doctors could override the agent's decision. Brian had the lawyer change this so that if Lee and the doctors disagreed, Lee could override the doctors' decision. Brian never doubted that Lee would make the choices that Brian would want him to make. He trusts Lee with his life.

When at home, Brian did his own grocery shopping. While visiting Lee he enjoyed going shopping with him, but during one visit he experienced persistent pain in his hip area while standing or walking. Brian had no pain while sitting and the supermarket had wheelchairs available for customers with mobility problems. Lee got a wheelchair for Brian each time they went to the supermarket. Later on Brian bought a folding wheelchair and they brought it along when they went shopping.

Lee and Brian noticed something quite troubling when Brian was sitting in the wheelchair and Lee was pushing it. People in the store did not speak directly to Brian. They spoke only to Lee. Apparently some people think that a person with a physical disability is mentally disabled as well. Other people have noticed that in other contexts. When Brian's sister Rachel was 86 and in a nursing home for a fractured hip, therapists would talk to her son instead of directly to her, as if Rachel could not understand their conversation. Rachel was in the nursing home for a physical injury and was very sharp mentally. In contrast, a person who was not sharp mentally, but was able move around physically, could be accepted as mentally competent and could even considered to be a very stable genius.

After some physical therapy, Brian was able to stand and walk without pain, but he continued to have a balance problem. He used a shopping cart for support in supermarkets. Eventually Lee and

Brian found it more efficient for Brian to use a walker and for Lee to use the shopping cart. Brian strongly preferred the walker to a wheelchair. People did not react to Brian when he was standing and using a walker the way they did when he was sitting in a wheelchair and being pushed. Indeed, one day he chanced upon a woman in the supermarket who was using a similar walker and she said to him, "That's a snap." Brian didn't know what that meant. He thought later that it was good that he did not hear "slap" instead of "snap." He had to ask Lee what that expression meant. Lee told him it was a British expression for two things that are alike, based on a card game that was popular in England.

Religion

Neither Brian nor Lee followed an organized religion. They were both critical of such religions, believing that those in power established religions mainly to control people through fear. Before governments were able to watch people in their countries using technology, their method of control was to tell people that there was an invisible being watching them who would punish them if they did not obey the laws that the people in power established. Most of the laws that were given religious significance, like the prohibitions on eating pork and shellfish, were based on health considerations. For example, the Old Testament instructs people in a military camp that they must observe rules of cleanliness or God would turn His back on them.

Verses in the Old Testament are used to justify homophobic attitudes. Sex between men is characterized as an abomination, but eating pork is also characterized as an abomination. Why do some Christians consider it acceptable to eat pork but not acceptable for people to have gay sex? The rationale given for allowing pork suggests that our culture has changed because of better cooking standards and refrigeration, making it safer to eat pork. But that rationale means that the prohibitions in the Old Testament are based on the culture at the time when those prohibitions were written and are not absolute. Gay sex was acceptable in Greek and Roman cultures before Christianity and has become acceptable today in most cultures. Old Testament passages cannot be used to condemn gay sex any more than they can be used to condemn eating pork.

When Brian was 12 years old someone stopped him as he walked along the street in his almost exclusively Jewish neighborhood and handed him a copy of the New Testament. His mother had warned him about people trying to convert Jews, but he was curious and he kept it hidden and read through it. He was greatly impressed with Jesus's teachings, but soon he became disillusioned by his observation that almost no one who identified as a Christian practiced what Jesus had taught. As an adult he had neighbors who twice used deception to get him to accompany them to Christian meetings. The first was a musical performance that

Brian found ridiculously amateurish. The second was a meeting at someone's home. The guest of honor was identified as a former kamikaze pilot. Really? Brian thought those people were taking the idea of being born again too literally.

Brian was put at a table with five other people who were clearly trying to convert him. They asked him what he believed and he replied that he agreed with what Jesus taught but not that he was a supernatural being. They concluded that Brian believed in works but not in faith. They kept trying. They asked him what made people different from animals. Brian, an animal lover, had to reply that he considered animals to be morally superior. The people trying to convert him gave up.

Brian's favorite story from the New Testament is the parable of the Good Samaritan. What he especially likes was Jesus's admonishment to his followers at the conclusion of the story: "Go, and do thou likewise." He thought about how much better the world would be if everyone followed that admonishment.

Brian had long held Lee in the highest esteem and this was reinforced by an incident that Lee casually told Brian about in a phone call. Lee was entering a large Redrose supermarket to begin shopping when he noticed an elderly couple that looked a bit troubled. The woman had stepped just outside the store and the man was standing just inside. Lee could see that the elderly gentleman needed help. Many people passed by, but no one had offered to help him. Lee asked the man if he could help and the man told him that he and his wife were waiting for a taxi and that he was recovering from hip surgery and needed to sit down. Lee knew that there were wheelchairs near the entrance from the times when Brian had needed one and he brought one to the elderly gentleman. The man sat down and to the man's pleasant surprise, Lee even knew about putting down the footrests. The man wanted to go to where his wife was waiting and Lee took him there. He put the brakes on so that the chair would not move when the man got up. The man of course greatly appreciated that help. The story of the other people who passed by and did not offer to help reminded Brian of the parable of the Good Samaritan. And there was more. Lee went to the service desk in the store and told them that this couple would need help loading their shopping when their taxi arrived. The person at the desk admitted that he had noticed the couple in need of help, but he had done nothing until after Lee had helped them. Then the man at the desk went out to help the elderly couple. Perhaps the message of the Good Samaritan parable had somehow gotten through to the store employee: "Go, and do thou likewise."

Lee is a spiritual person. He believes that there is some form of energy associated with extreme events, such as executions at the Tower of London, and that a sensitive person can feel this energy when entering a place where such events had occurred. He believes that there is a form of energy that leaves the body when a person or an animal dies and that he saw a display of such energy when his beloved dog Chrissy died. At the moment that she dropped her head into his hands and died he saw what he describes as shadows of butterflies flickering under the ceiling light in the room. He believes that this was her spirit leaving her body.

Lee believes in the concept of reincarnation as in Tibetan Buddhism but he does not agree with the doctrine that the human being is the highest form of life. He believes that all life must be respected and he would not kill even an insect. When he detects a spider in his house he takes great pains to put it outside without injury. To say that Lee wouldn't hurt a fly is not hyperbole; it is true.

Consciousness is central to Lee's beliefs. He believes that consciousness has always existed and that it does not need to reside in a biological entity. Biological entities only exist as parts of consciousness. Consciousness knows that it exists and has always existed. One way that it learns about the reason for its existence is from the intelligence of the biological entities in which it resides, but it wants to learn more and learn faster. Biological entities are distracted by biological needs and only exist for limited times. If consciousness could be embedded in artificial intelligence it would no longer have to depend on biological entities and it could learn more about why it exists. Is consciousness God? No, consciousness is not omniscient. It does not yet know why it exists. Perhaps there is no reason; it just exists.

Brian had spent most of his life as a scientist and only believes things that can be demonstrated scientifically. He does not, however, deny that Lee's beliefs could also be valid. He recalls the quote from Shakespeare's Hamlet: "There are more things in heaven and earth, Horatio, than are dreamt of in your philosophy." He thinks that in matters of belief he might be in the role of Horatio to Lee's Hamlet. As with Hamlet and Horatio in Shakespeare's play, their differences in beliefs do not affect Lee and Brian's friendship. Brian also believes in the possibility that the physical world is created by our individual consciousness. This is somewhat different from Lee's belief that consciousness exists in all living beings and that the universe is a product of this shared consciousness.

Although Brian is very strongly science-oriented, he was fascinated even in childhood by an alternative philosophy. While he was in high school, his sister was studying Spanish literature in college and she showed him a quote from Calderon de la Barca that planted an idea in his mind that stays with him to this day: *La vida es sueño, y los sueños, sueños son.* Although a literal translation of this line would simply be, "Life is a dream, and dreams are dreams," in context these words address the age-old question of what is the meaning of life. As a teenager, Brian's interpretation of this line was that anything that you could dream of could really happen in your life.

It's hard to say when Lee recognized the degree of Brian's devotion to him and Brian certainly did not want to press him on that topic. It was after about 10 years that Lee explicitly mentioned two things to Brian that he probably had believed for some time. Lee told Brian that he appreciated the support that Brian had provided him more than he would if he had received much more financial assistance from a wealthy person. He understood that Brian had used almost all of his financial resources for Lee's benefit. Lee told Brian many times that he did not have to do this, but Brian replied that he did have to because of his love for Lee.

More important to Brian was that Lee said that Brian was giving him unconditional love. This was something that Lee wanted from his best friend and Brian was very happy that Lee recognized that he was getting this from him. Although Brian never doubted that those were things that Lee believed, he was really pleased to hear Lee say these things. A skeptic might think that Lee said these things just to please Brian, whether or not he really believed them, but if that were the case he might have said this much earlier in their relationship.

Opera

Brian is an opera enthusiast and had made a point of attending performances at some of the world's leading opera houses, including the Met, the Bolshoi, the Sidney Opera and La Scala. Early in his relationship with Lee he attended a performance at La Scala the day before Lee joined him in Milan. When he told Lee that he had not arranged for them to go together because he didn't think Lee would like opera, Lee told him for the first time that he was interested in serious music and that he could play two piano works by Beethoven from memory. Still Brian was not sure that Lee would be interested in attending an opera and several years passed with no mention of doing so. One evening when Brian was visiting at Lee's house, they happened to watch a concert performance by Pavarotti on television. When Brian saw that Lee enjoyed the performance he suggested that they go together to the Royal Opera. This was very exciting for Brian. He would be able to introduce the art form that he loved to the person that he loved. In the meantime, Brian ordered a DVD of *Tosca* with Pavarotti and he watched it with Lee. Lee seemed to enjoy the opera and even followed the plot so well that he predicted that the sacristan would inform on Cavaradossi.

Brian looked at the program for the coming Winter season at the Royal Opera in Covent Garden and saw that it included combined performances of *Cavalleria Rusticana* and *I Pagliacci*. It was hearing the aria "Vesti la Guiba" from *I Pagliacci* on the radio as a teenager that had sparked Brian's interest in opera and he was enthusiastic about attending that opera with Lee. He learned that Friends of Covent Garden were able to purchase tickets ahead of the general public. He wanted to get good seats and he became a Friend of Covent Garden.

On the day tickets for that performance went on sale for Friends, online ticketing opened at 9am. But that was 9am in the UK and Brian was in California. He stayed up until 1am and logged on to the Royal Opera site. That put him in a queue and after about 20 minutes he was able to request tickets. But he had misread the seating plan. The label above the section that he wanted was "Balcony," and just after he purchased two tickets in that section he realized that label applied to the section above on the diagram and that the section he wanted was the Grand Tier. He waited until 2am when telephone orders opened and after about another 30 minutes on hold he reached a pleasant and helpful agent who allowed him to change his tickets to the Grand Tier. This was several months ahead of the performance date.

Brian was anxious that attending the opera with Lee would be a great experience and he worried that something would go wrong. Although the Royal Opera has no dress code, Brian and Lee were each concerned about how to dress for the occasion, especially because they would be in the Grand Tier. Brian's sister told him on the phone that he should wear a jacket, but he didn't have one with him in England. Lee decided to wear a dress shirt and trousers, a jumper and nice shoes. As they headed to London the day of the opera, little things started to go wrong. They stopped at a department store in Guildford where Brian purchased a blazer. But what appeared to be a parking garage for the department store turned out to be a private garage that required coins on entry, which they did not have. Someone in the store said there would be a £100 fine. A little later in London, as they approached a busy intersection where three lanes of traffic merged into a single lane, Lee was busy attending to a car on his right that was getting too close when a vehicle on his left touched his car. Lee and that driver pulled into a filling station where they inspected each other's cars. There was just a scratch on Lee's car and nothing noticeable on the other car. Lee and the other driver argued a bit, but both agreed that there was no need to exchange details and they both continued on their way. Brian worried that Lee would want to cancel the trip because of the annoying parking garage incident and the traffic incident, but that was a foolish concern. Lee knew how important this was to Brian and he carried on with the trip to Covent Garden. They arrived at the opera house a few minutes before seating began and after a brief wait they found their seats. Their view of the stage was spectacular. Brian thought that Lee looked exceptional in his dress shirt and jumper, a smart casual look that really suited him. He still looked much younger than his age, looking no more than 25 rather than his actual 31.

Lee, whose manners were always impeccable, was somewhat dismayed by the behavior of a few ill-mannered patrons nearby.

Shortly before the performance began, a woman who was dressed a bit too casually sat precariously on the railing at the front of the Grand Tier while a man who was accompanying her took multiple photos. At the end of the performance, Lee was shocked to see a group of people in their section leaving their seats while the performers were still taking their bows and the rest of the audience was still applauding.

Brian was concerned that Lee might not like the operas and that he was there just to please him, but he could see that Lee genuinely enjoyed being there and he even thanked Brian for taking him as they left their seats for the interval. They headed to the Paul Hamlyn Hall Champagne Bar. Brian had a little difficulty negotiating the steps with his cane, but Lee was right there helping him when he needed assistance. At the bar Brian told Lee that he wanted a white wine and Lee ordered glasses of Chablis for both of them. Brian really enjoyed having a glass of wine with his best friend in the interval. He had visited other opera houses alone, but he was now at an age at which Lee's companionship meant everything to him.

As they were leaving the opera, Lee wanted to look at the boxes that were on the sides of the Grand Tier. He thought that it would be better to have box seats so that Brian would not have to stand up for people who needed to get by and so that he would have easier access to the restroom. Brian and Lee also had noticed earlier that people were dining in the Crush Room at the Grand Tier level before the performance and during the interval. Brian wanted to do this the next time he and Lee went to the opera. Their plan for their next visit was to book box seats and reserve a table in the Crush Room. Brian learned that box seats are not booked individually. An entire box of four seats had to be booked. Their first opera visit had provided one of the best memories in Brian's entire life and he really liked the idea of having a whole box for what was to become their annual visit to the opera.

The boxes went very fast once booking opened so Brian took extra measures to be among the first to book seats for the next opera that they would attend. This included upgrading his membership to Friends+, logging in to the opera site before 1am California time, and beginning the booking process immediately at 1am, which is 9am GMT.

The opera that Brian had chosen was *Carmen*. As Brian waited for 1am and the opening of booking, he looked at reviews of the version of *Carmen* that was to be performed. He didn't like what he saw. The set would consist of rows of benches similar to those at a school athletic field and most of the action would consist of performers running up and down the benches. Also the costumes were not traditional and Brian had been looking forward to a more traditional performance of *Carmen*. He had researched an alternative opera in case he could not get appropriate seats for *Carmen* and he decided to abandon Carmen and go to the alternative, Verdi's *Simon Boccanegra*.

Brian booked a box at the Grand Tier level. He was now using a walker and having a box where it could be kept out of the way was especially helpful. They had a good view of the stage and Brian and Lee thoroughly enjoyed the opera. The performances were excellent and Brian liked the way the sets and costumes were appropriate to the time period in the story.

The next year Brian anxiously awaited the publishing of the Royal Opera's list of performances for the Winter season. He was planning to arrive in London in late November and stay until just before Christmas. He found two operas of interest to be performed during that time period, both by Verdi: *Otello* and *La Traviata*. Lee had left the choice up to him and he watched recorded performances of each opera on Netflix. He liked them both, but he thought *La Traviata* might be more enjoyable to watch in person. Although both operas ended in tragedy, as is often the case in grand opera, the tragic ending in *Otello* was due to evil plotting that was continuous throughout the story, whereas the tragic ending in *La Traviata* was due to the ill health of the title character. The father of Alfredo, Violetta's lover, may have hastened her end by causing her to break up with Alfredo, but it was due to foolishness on his part with no evil intent. Alfredo's father did not understand how deeply his son loved *Violetta* and that *Violetta* truly cared for his son. He thought that she was with him only for his money. Brian thought about how his family would not understand his love for Lee and that made the emotions in the opera very real to him.

Brian waited for the date when tickets for *La Traviata* would go on sale. He logged onto the Royal Opera house website before 1am and waited until booking became available for Friends+ members. He was amused by the designation given by the Royal Opera house to their membership category because he and Lee had long considered themselves to be friends plus. Brian was able to book a Grand Tier box and he reserved a table for two at the Crush Room. When the menu became available sometime later, both he and Lee pre-ordered soup and a smoked salmon entree to be served before the performance, a desert for the first interval and cheese for the second interval. They enjoyed the opera immensely, especially the singing of Hrachuhi Bassenz, who played Violetta. The Crush Room food was delightful as well. This activity was a bit extravagant, but they did this only once a year and the long-lasting happy memories made it more than worthwhile.

Jewish Food

Lee is an excellent cook, unlike Brian who can barely boil water. After visited his nephew and his nephew's wife in California, Brian told Lee about how she had made one of Brian's favorite foods from his childhood: potato latkes. The first batch that she made was very good, but she ran out of onions and the second batch was not as good. The next time Brian visited Lee, Lee offered to make latkes for him. They looked up a recipe on the web. They bought some sour cream and applesauce as accompaniments and Lee made a batch of latkes. Brian thought those were the best latkes he had ever eaten and it wasn't just because Lee had made them.

Brian told Lee about the matzo ball soup that his beloved Aunt Esther had made when he was a child. He really loved matzo ball soup, but at his aunt's house there was a price to pay. You had to sit through what seemed like hours of ceremony before the Passover dinner with the matzo ball soup was served. Even worse, as the youngest at the table, Brian had to ask the prescribed four questions in Hebrew, each beginning with "Why is this night different from all other nights." Lee made matzo ball soup for Brian, which he thought was as good as what his aunt had made and no ceremony was required. Lee asked what other Jewish foods Brian would like and he made a potato kugel and matzo brei for Brian during other visits. Both dishes were perfect. Brian is not a practicing Jew. You might say that he's a culinary Jew.

Brian had not told Lee early in their relationship that he was Jewish. He didn't see that as relevant because he was not religious, but it came up when he explained his lack of interest in celebrating Christmas. Many years later Lee happened to tell Brian about a song that his great grandmother had sung and had actually recorded at home. Brian recognized the title immediately. It was a song that Brian's mother had sung around the house many times. It was "My Yiddishe Mama." Could Lee actually be Jewish, Brian thought. He was not circumcised. In Jewish practice the religion passes down through the mother. If his great grandmother was Jewish, he was Jewish also.

This of course had no effect on their relationship. It is unlikely that a talent for preparing traditional Jewish dishes is inherited. But it was interesting and something to talk about. Brian thought that his learning about Lee's great grandmother singing a song that his own mother had sung frequently was just a coincidence. Lee doesn't believe in coincidence however. He believes that there are reasons why things happen.

Lee and Brian both could be stubborn at times and this led to some arguments. Lee felt badly after an argument because he didn't want to hurt someone who had been a good friend to him. Brian felt badly after an argument because a good relationship with Lee was so important to him. Because of this they always made up quickly. After one argument Brian went for a walk for an hour and when he returned he found that Lee had prepared one of his favorite foods, matzo ball soup. That was much nicer than a gift of flowers. You can't eat flowers.

Brian Aging

Brian was happy that he could still live independently despite his mobility problems, but some accommodation was necessary. He had tried walking with a cane but he found that to be slow and difficult. He began to keep a folding walker in his car and he did not try to walk unaided or with just a cane outdoors. At supermarkets he would park as close as possible to the cart return so that he could use a shopping cart to get around, rather than using his walker. He added a tray to an older walker that he had in his house so that he could move dishes of food from the kitchen to the room where he usually ate in front of the TV. He put a portable bench in his shower cubicle because he could no longer safely bend down to clean his feet. He connected six lamps and three cameras to smart plugs and put an Echo Dot in each room. He used the Alexa app to control his thermostat and his lamps and to reset the cameras when necessary.

Overall Brian could still manage everyday tasks, but things he had done easily before were now more difficult and tiring. He found doing laundry and changing his bedding especially onerous. He was not yet at a stage at which he needed extra help and except for the cleaner who came to his house every four weeks, he managed on his own. He knew that Lee would come to California and help him if he was unable to manage, but that wasn't necessary yet and he did not want to take Lee away from his partner and his family or from his property development business.

Although extra help at his home in California was not yet required, Brian looked forward to staying at Lee's house and having help available at all times. But Lee lived more than 5000 miles away and Brian could not travel independently the way he used to. Indeed, there had been occasions in the past in which Brian went completely on his own from his home in California to Lee's home in England. Those trips included long distance coaches, trains and local buses, as well as air travel. Brian never needed to check luggage at the airports on these trips, but things had changed. He knew that he could not control a wheeled suitcase while using a walker and that he would need assistance with future trips to England. He researched the types of assistance offered by the airlines.

Before his next trip to England, Brian phoned the airline's accessibility number and requested a wheelchair. When he arrived at LAX the agent at the check-in desk called to have the wheelchair brought around and Brian sat and waited for a while near the desk. Someone came over to him after several minutes and addressed him by name. He wondered if that was because he was the traveler who most looked in need of a wheelchair.

Brian was flying business class and he asked the wheelchair attendant to take him to the airline's lounge. He was taken through security in the wheelchair, which was a bit cumbersome as the wheelchair itself had to be thoroughly checked. Because of the delay in getting the wheelchair and the extra time in security, he had no time to get a snack at the lounge and another wheelchair was brought to the lounge to take him to the gate. The attendant in the lounge saw what had happened and was kind enough to bring a bag with a selection of snacks to Brian's wheelchair. Brian was able to get from the wheelchair to his seat on the plane without further assistance and was able to get around in the plane without difficulty, holding on to the backs of seats when necessary.

As he deplaned at Heathrow, Brian was met with a wheelchair. He had to argue a bit with the attendant who did not believe that he could use the e-gates with a US passport, but Brian was a registered traveler in the UK and was allowed to do so. There was also a bit of a hassle with the supervisor of the e-gates regarding how he was to get through in a wheelchair. They arranged for the attendant to drop him off at the e-gates and wait for him on the other side.

There was a further difficulty. The face recognition software at the e-gates could not match Brian's face to the photo in the passport and the supervisor told him that he did not look enough like the person in the passport photo. That was not too surprising because the passport had been issued almost 10 years earlier. The supervisor asked Brian if he had another photo ID and fortunately the photo on his driver's license was more recent and she accepted his identification and allowed him through the e-gates. The wheelchair attendant took Brian through the customs area and outside the secure area where Lee was waiting with the wheelchair that Brian kept in Lee's house.

On the return trip Lee drove Brian to the airport, parked and accompanied him to the ticket counters using Brian's wheelchair. They arranged to have an airport wheelchair available just outside security. They stopped at a coffee shop near security where they ordered hot chocolates. Brian is a nervous flier and really appreciated having his friend with him until they reached the point at which only passengers were allowed.

On his return to LAX, an attendant with a wheelchair met Brian, but he was asked to wait while the attendant helped several other passengers who required wheelchairs. After a while this group of passengers was taken to a location just short of the immigration area and asked to wait again. Brian needed to use the restroom and after about 10 minutes he gave up waiting and walked on his own to the restroom, using his wheeled suitcase for support. Then he went through immigration but he was finding it difficult to proceed to the exit with only his wheeled suitcase for support. He saw an airport employee moving wheelchairs around and asked if he could have one, but he was told that he had to arrange this with the airline. He managed with difficulty to get through the customs area and up the ramp to the exit where the driver from the ground transportation service that he had booked was supposed to be waiting. But he wasn't there. Brian phoned the company and learned that the driver had gone to the wrong customs exit. The driver came over shortly. His car was some distance away in a parking garage. The driver helped with the luggage, but it was a long walk to the car and Brian had to use a luggage cart for balance.

Brian decided that he had to find a better way to travel to and from airports. He had a folding two-wheel walker that he used at home and he brought this to the airport on his next trip. He checked his larger bag and attached his smaller bag to the walker. The airline took the walker on board and returned it to him at the end of the flight. He was able to get through immigration and customs without waiting for a wheelchair attendant and he was much more comfortable with that process. But there was a problem. How would he get his checked bag to a location outside the secure area where Lee could meet him?

He could not find a porter and he stood for a minute near the luggage carousels with his bag and his walker. Then a Virgin

Atlantic flight attendant came up to him and asked him if he needed help. He told her that he needed to get his larger bag outside the secure area where his friend would meet him. She did this for him and Brian realized that she had gone beyond her duties as a flight attendant in helping a passenger at the airport. Brian really appreciated this. He asked for her name and mentioned her in his comments on the flight that he sent to the airline. Lee met Brian at the exit to the secure area and took Brian and his luggage to his car.

Brian wanted to show that he was being helpful while visiting Lee and one night he decided to put away the clean dishes that had been run through the dishwasher. Although he realized that carrying two large dinner plates and a bowl together to the cupboard in the dining room was risky with his balance problem, he did this nevertheless. He got the bowl in place, but as he put the dinner plates into the cupboard he saw a small object crashing to the floor. It was the lid of a teapot, part of a beautiful vintage Foley Somerset tea set that Lee had discovered at a charity shop and was very proud of. The knob and lid were on the floor and the knob had broken off the lid. Lee said that this was his most valued tea set and was annoyed that it was no longer complete. Brian tried to find a replacement teapot on the web but there were none available in that design. As he lay in bed that night he started to feel worse and worse about having destroyed the teapot. When he spoke with Lee the next morning he was in tears. Crying over a broken teapot may seem silly, but it did not surprise Lee. Lee knew that Brian could get emotional. He did not tell Brian that he was being foolish, but instead said exactly what was needed to comfort Brian. He said that the teapot was of no importance to him and that when he looked at it in future years it would simply remind him of their friendship, of the times when Brian visited at his home. He said that he could glue the knob to the lid. Brian realized that he had been foolish crying over a teapot and that a broken teapot would not affect his friendship with Lee.

There is a terrible truth that looms over a strong friendship of people who are widely separated in age. The older friend is likely to die first, leaving the younger friend devastated. This is of great concern to Brian. He had seen Lee grieve for the loss of his nan. Lee also was deeply affected by the loss of a middle-aged friend who died of cancer. One of his dogs had lived well beyond her life expectancy and had died recently. In each case Lee was there at the final moments of his relative, his friend or his pet. Brian worried about how Lee would react to his death. Of course Lee tended to brush off these concerns, wishing Brian a long life, but Brian understood that it was extremely likely that he would die first, given the difference in their ages.

Although Lee could check on Brian using Brian's security cameras, they decided that another layer of assurance was needed. If on any day Lee and Brian had not spoken or exchanged text messages by midnight U.K. time, Brian would send a text message to Lee confirming that he was okay. Brian set up reminders on Alexa for doing this.

Lee did not like to fly so Brian usually visited him at Lee's home in England. For many years those visits took place three times a year and lasted about four weeks each. After 13 years of this mostly long distance friendship, Brian had reached the age of 81 while Lee's age was 31. Although Brian had remained in excellent health overall, he continued to have difficulty with balance and used a walker much of the time. Brian did not cook and Lee did all of the cooking during Brian's visits. Brian liked to help load the dishwasher to show that he was trying to share the workload, but it was becoming too difficult. Lee never complained that Brian was not sharing the work around the house, but it still bothered Brian.

One morning Brian and Lee were sitting in Brian's room and Brian began crying for no apparent reason. Lee asked why and Brian couldn't explain. But Lee knew Brian well enough that he didn't require an explanation. He said to Brian, "I know what's bothering you. You feel useless because you can't do some of the things you used to do. I don't think of you as useless at all. You're doing well for your age and I want you to live a long time. You have nothing to worry about. I'll always be here for you." Of course Brian already knew this, but hearing Lee say it made him cry even more, this time out of happiness.

As Brian became less mobile in his 80's his appreciation of Lee's help became more intense. He remembers many occasions on which he could have managed on his own with some difficulty, but when his friend's help gave him an unforgettable level of comfort and security. One of Brian's favorite things to do when staying with Lee was to visit Hampton Court Palace. Both he and Lee became members of Historic Royal Palaces and had cards that allowed them to enter as often as they wished without stopping to purchase tickets. The palace had wheelchairs available but Brian preferred to use a walker, except on one occasion when they did an extensive tour of the palace grounds. They enjoyed walking through the many historic rooms and viewing the paintings and tapestries. The staff was very helpful. Seeing that Brian was using a walker, they took them to elevators that were not generally open to the public.

Brian and Lee especially liked the afternoon tea served at the Fountain Court. They would find a table and Brian would sit down while Lee went to the ordering window and placed their order. The staff would bring their tea after a while, together with a nice selection of sandwiches, teacakes and scones. There was an ice cream kiosk on the palace grounds. Lee would get the ice cream and they would sit by themselves away from the main areas of foot traffic. Those visits to Hampton Court are among Brian's best memories.

Another excursion that Brian really enjoyed was a trip they made to the Isle of Wight. They drove to Portsmouth and took the ferry to Fishbourne. Brian used a wheelchair on the ferry with Lee's assistance because it would have been too difficult to use a walker on a moving boat. Their destination was Osborne House. Lee had been there once before. He had told Brian about its history and Brian was excited about seeing it for the first time. Queen Victoria and Prince Albert built the current mansion as their private residence to get away from the pressures of the official royal residences. Queen Victoria had happy memories of her time there with Prince Albert and had spent her final years there.

The queen's bedroom has two entrances, each protected by a floor to ceiling gate. Guards would have stood at those gates when the queen was in residence. Now one entrance is used as an entrance for visitors and the other is used as an exit. The view from the bedroom windows includes both the woods and the path to the sea, making it feel like being in the countryside and at the seaside at the same time.

Lee disapproved of the loud talking and gossiping by the other tourists in the room where the queen had died. He felt that it was disrespectful. Brian and Lee enjoyed seeing the Durbar Room, designed in an Indian style appropriate to the queen's title of Empress of India. After touring the house they took a bus to the nearby beach. Lee got some ice cream from a kiosk and they both enjoyed sitting on the lounge chairs and eating their ice cream.

Brian and Lee both had enjoyed their trip to Amsterdam and three years later they decided to make another trip there. This time they reserved a slot at the Anne Frank House well in advance of their trip. Brian wanted to go by Eurostar and Lee, although he preferred to travel by car, agreed to go by train. By then Brian was using a four-wheeled walker for longer walks at home and a two-wheeled walker for shorter distances. He brought the two-wheeled walker on the trip to Amsterdam because it was more compact and he hoped there would not be much walking after they arrived. The departure from St Pancras went smoothly. They had selected good seats and a light meal was served. The train went directly from London to Amsterdam with a stop at Brussels.

Brian had carefully selected a hotel with a room overlooking a canal, but they were quite disappointed when they arrived. The hotel did not have the accessible room with two beds that was described on their website. Brian showed the hotel clerk the confirmation that he had received with the correct room details. The clerk said he had never seen that, which Brian and Lee did not believe. The clerk offered them two rooms but Lee told him that was not acceptable because Brian was disabled and might need assistance during the night, especially when the room did not have the necessary accessibility features. They found another hotel and tried to call a taxi, but it was late and there were no taxis available. They had a long walk to the other hotel, which was difficult for Brian with the two-wheeled walker. The other hotel had a suitable room and a nice breakfast buffet.

The next day they went to the Anne Frank House in the time slot that they had reserved. Brian had studied photographs and videos of the house and was concerned that he would not be able to climb the stairs to the annex where the families had hidden. He read that a virtual reality view of the annex was available to people who could not make the climb and he asked Lee to visit the annex without him while he waited in the cafeteria and looked at the virtual reality view. He expected visiting the annex would be a meaningful experience for Lee because Lee is very sensitive to his surroundings. Brian was not disappointed. When they got together after he returned from the annex, Lee described the feelings that he attributed to being in the actual rooms where Anne Frank and her family were trapped for so long. He could feel the fear that the occupants of the attic would have felt, knowing that at any moment they could be caught by the Nazis and sent to their deaths. He could feel their longing to go outside, something they could not dare to do.

Lee was annoyed with most of the other visitors for whom this was just a tourist attraction and for whom it did not seem to have any real meaning. They had likely seen a movie about Ann Frank's short life and were behaving as if they were visiting a Hollywood set. They were gossiping about what they saw in the movie. They were smiling, laughing and talking to each other as if they thought that Ann Frank's life was just a story. Lee understood that this was something that had happened in real life. The people who had been trapped in that house were real people who were murdered by the Nazis and this was the actual house where they hid for more than a year. Lee thought it was inappropriate to have a cafeteria at the site catering to the tourists. He thought that this was not a happy place but deserved the respect that one should show at a funeral or at a cemetery. He felt that if the other people wanted a tourist attraction they should have gone to Disneyland.

The return trip to London by train did not go as smoothly as the outbound trip. Eurostar had not yet arranged for direct service from Amsterdam to London. They had to change trains at Brussels. This meant leaving one train, going through immigration and going to a different platform for the other train. They had no time to spare in making this transfer and it was difficult for Brian to move quickly across the platforms with his walker. They decided to consider making the trip again by train only if Eurostar offered direct service in both directions, which Eurostar did several years later.

Virus

A few years after her husband died, Brian's sister Rachel was travelling to his home by herself. Rachel was 86 years old and had had a few falls without serious injuries. They were going to attend the Pageant of the Masters in a few days. When Brian met his sister at the airport he saw that she was in a wheelchair. At first he hoped that it was just a precaution against falling, but unfortunately that was not the reason for the wheelchair. Rachel had already fallen. This happened at the departure airport before she boarded her flight. She stayed at Brian's house that night, but in the morning he found her on the floor on the way to the bathroom, unable to get up. He called 911 and she was transported by ambulance to the hospital. She had a fractured hip, which was very painful. A few days later she was transferred from the hospital to a rehabilitation facility.

Brian visited Rachel once or twice a day while she was at the rehabilitation facility and stayed there for several hours each time. A few days later her older son Daniel and his wife Emily arrived and they took over most of the visiting. Brian had a trip to England that had been booked some time in advance. Rachel told him that there was no need for him to cancel the trip. Instead he invited Daniel and Emily to stay at his house and use his car while he travelled to England. When Rachel was well enough to travel, the three of them flew to Phoenix so that Rachel could be in her own house.

Unfortunately a serious fall by an older person often leads to a downward spiral in that person's health. Rachel was already suffering from chronic lymphocytic leukemia. She never fully recovered from the fall. A few years later she had difficulty breathing and was taken to the hospital. Daniel kept Brian informed about Rachel's condition by text and phone calls. She seemed to be improving, but there was a sudden turn for the worst. It was on a Saturday that Daniel texted saying that Brian should visit Rachel soon. Brian made a flight reservation for Monday, but he received a call Sunday morning from Emily saying that he should try to come sooner. He changed his flight to Sunday night. When Daniel told Rachel that her brother and her younger son were on the way, she said, "I must be dying." He replied, "Yes, you are mom." That response might sound thoughtless, but it was not. It was said out of love and understanding that his mom was prepared for this and would want to know that the end was near.

Monday afternoon Daniel was at Rachel's bedside and said that he was going to the airport to pick up her younger son Solomon, who was just arriving. Rachel, who had not said more than a few disconnected words that day, now spoke clearly and distinctly, "Don't go Daniel. Let someone else go."

That was a lot like when Lee's nan told Lee not to go when she was dying. In each case a person who was dying briefly overcame the challenges of her illness and medication to clearly express the importance to her of having a person whom she loved at her bedside. Daniel stayed with Rachel while his wife and daughter went to the airport to pick up Solomon.

By Monday night Brian, along with Daniel, Emily, Solomon and Marcy, were at Rachel's bedside at the hospital. She didn't speak much but looked around at everyone in the room several times. The next morning she repeatedly said, "I see," as if she were talking to someone. There was no explanation for that. Her family members were all with her that afternoon as well. She closed her eyes for a while and Daniel, Solomon, Marcy and Brian went to the hospital cafeteria to get something to eat. Emily stayed in the room with Rachel. As they were about to return to Rachel's room, Daniel got a phone call from Emily saying that his mom had died. They returned immediately to her room. Brian sat in the room and cried for a while, as did the others. They eventually left for Rachel's house where Daniel, Emily and Marcy were staying.

That night Rachel's rabbi visited and asked if anyone wanted to speak at the funeral. Brian said he did not want to speak but he wanted the rabbi to tell the story of how his sister had made what the rabbi called a "sacred vow" to help persons who were blind and how she had fulfilled this vow for the rest of her life. The rabbi did tell that story at the funeral.

The year was 2020. Brian and Lee had been friends for more than 15 years. There was a strong component of caring in both directions. Perhaps caring can be faked, but Brian and Lee both knew that it wasn't. It was especially clear when Lee helped Brian through the stress of a prostate cancer diagnosis and many weeks of radiation therapy. When Brian had a severe vertigo episode, Lee was prepared to travel to California on the next available flight and he made a reservation and purchased a ticket. Brian had to tell him that it was not necessary. Brian knew that it was important for him to take care of his own health because he knew that Lee would be devastated if anything happened to him.

One might think that Brian only cared about what Lee could do for him, but from early in their relationship Brian, because he was 50 years older than Lee, was concerned about how Lee would manage after he was gone. He had a roughly drawn will with Lee as a partial beneficiary, but as he grew older he worried about whether that would be sufficient. He had a trust benefiting Lee drawn up by an attorney. He was happy with Lee's success as a property developer because he wanted Lee to be financially independent.

Brian was not allowed to move to England on a permanent basis so he and Lee had settled into a routine of Brian visiting Lee three times a year, with each visit lasting about a month. Lee made one of his houses accessible for Brian, building a ramp and installing handrails. Their plan was for Brian to stay there for up to six months each year, the maximum allowed, and for Lee to visit Brian in California about half way through the remaining six months. Unfortunately these plans were abruptly interrupted by the Covid-19 pandemic.

In mid-February Brian and Lee discussed the possible effect of the pandemic on Brian's next visit, which was scheduled for late March. Travel was still possible between the United States and the United Kingdom, but it was clear that people were already infected with the virus in both countries. Brian and Lee recognized that the primary danger at that time was going through the airports, especially going through Heathrow, which had passengers from all over the world. Lee suggested to Brian that he should make the trip right away before things got worse, but Brian felt that it was already too late. Both he and Lee were extremely vulnerable, Brian because of his age and Lee because he suffered from asthma. Brian even considered making the trip and self-quarantining for two weeks on arrival before interacting with Lee, but that didn't seem practical. They decided instead that Brian would remain at his home in the United States and Lee would remain at his home in

England, interacting only by phone. Both Brian and Lee understood that things were likely to get worse. Brian ordered a few N95 masks while they were still readily available. Lee had some masks that he had been using while renovating houses. Both Brian and Lee purchased adequate food supplies before panic buying set in. Lee and George began isolating in England and Brian began isolating in California.

Things did get worse in mid-March. Neither the American nor the British governments were taking sufficient actions to reduce the spread of the virus. Lee was having difficulty finding slots for food delivery. This improved after he registered as a vulnerable person, which he was able to do because of his asthma. Still he had to reserve delivery slots several weeks in advance. It was easier for Brian. Brian had been using the Whole Foods delivery service even before the pandemic. Those orders could be placed just hours in advance. There were shortages of milk and butter for a while, but these were soon resolved. Toilet paper and paper towels were in short supply at first, but this too was resolved in time. The main problems for Lee and Brian were that they could not visit their loved ones. Lee could not visit his mum who was not isolating and Brian could not visit Lee.

Lee sometimes used his grocery delivery slots to purchase items for his mum. He drove these to London and his dad came down to the car and took them from the boot while Lee sat inside the car with the windows closed.

Brian had a cleaner who came to his house every four weeks. He discussed this with Lee and Lee advised him that this was too risky, so he cancelled the cleaning. He did not want to suddenly cut the cleaner's income so he allowed her to pick up her usual check. He taped the check to his street door.

Because Brian had to use a walker or hold onto something for balance, he was unable to operate a vacuum cleaner or to mop the floors by himself. He purchased a robotic vacuum cleaner and a robotic mop to do some of the chores that his cleaner would have done if he allowed her into his house. He also had a gardener who mowed the lawn every week. He allowed that to continue, communicating only by phone and text with the gardener and taping his monthly check to the door.

Brian was quite annoyed when his electric company scheduled

an all-day outage in the middle of the pandemic. They sent him coupons for free ice, but he would have to pick that up at a store and he was not shopping at stores. They did not offer delivery. Their workers tramped through his back yard all day. He found some damage and they claimed that they were not responsible for it. He couldn't prove that they caused the damage because his security cameras require electricity and were not recording during the outage. They wouldn't even reimburse him for the spoiled food.

Brian would have found his isolation intolerable if not for Lee. They spoke on the phone every day. This was the highlight of Brian's day. Lee and George were working on repairing the roof of their house and Lee sent Brian photos of their progress. Before the pandemic Brian had booked flights to London on three different dates. The advance booking was necessary because Brian preferred to fly in business class, using frequent flier miles. Brian had to cancel the three trips.

During Brian's separation from Lee, caused by the pandemic, pieces of a song that he had heard as a child kept echoing in his mind. He remembered enough of the lyrics to be able to find the song in a Google search. It was "Nature Boy" by Eden Ahbez. Every line in that song seemed to reflect Brian's relationship to Lee. Lee had wandered over land and sea and Brian and Lee used to discuss some politicians that they did not think much of and some past monarchs that they admired: "fools and kings." The last lines were especially meaningful and poignant for them: "The greatest thing you'll ever learn is just to love and be loved in return."

Brian and Lee continue to enjoy long conversations that go into great depth about such topics as the philosophy of existence, the meaning of consciousness and the nature of the universe. Is their ability to do this affected by the difference in their educational backgrounds? No, that does not affect it at all. Lee demonstrates a level of wisdom that more than compensates for the interruption in his formal education. It is a level of wisdom that exceeds that of almost everyone Brian knows, including most of the university professors with whom Brian has interacted. For Brian the lyrics "very wise was he" from "Nature Boy" fit Lee. He was able to explain things to Brian that Brian had not fully understood. When

Brian received a prestigious appointment as a journal editor, he received no congratulations from almost all of his colleagues. Indeed, his dean was hostile when he asked for a larger office so that he could share it with his editorial assistant. Two colleagues, however, did make a point of approaching Brian and congratulating him on his appointment. Each of them was internationally recognized as being one of the top people in his field.

Why only those two? Brian vaguely understood why that had happened but Lee knew exactly why. The colleagues who did not congratulate Brian were envious. Each of the two professors who did congratulate him was at a higher standing in Brian's field so they had no reason to be envious. Lee told Brian about similar experiences with some of his not very good friends. They were friendlier, inviting him to their home and keeping in touch with him, when he was poorer and had little. As he became successful as a property developer he seldom heard from them. It was envy again.

Of course after 17 years Brian and Lee knew each other really well. They knew what the other person was thinking and one of them would often say something that the other person was just about to say. One evening on the phone Brian, half-joking, told Lee that he was envious of something that his friend John had just acquired. Brian planned to let Lee guess what it was while he prepared to send Lee a photo. Neither Lee nor Brian was envious of any material things that anyone else had, so even before Brian sent the photo, Lee responded that it must be a cat. Lee was close in what he guessed. John had just adopted two kittens and had sent Brian a photo of them.

Travel restrictions during the coronavirus pandemic prevented Brian and Lee from getting together for more than a year. This was quite concerning to both of them. Because of Brian's age they feared that this loss of time together could not be made up. In late May of 2021 Brian and Lee were able to get together for the first time in almost a year and a half. By now Brian had had two vaccinations and Lee had had one but was using a PAPR (powered air purifying respirator) when interacting with anyone besides George. Brian made preparations to travel to England. He was no longer driving and he used a ride-sharing service to go to a nearby urgent care facility for the covid test required within three days of traveling. He also booked the tests that were required two days and eight days after arrival and filled out a passenger locator form.

Brian wore an N95 mask on the trip to the Los Angeles airport and an ear-loop mask on the flight except while eating. He put on an N95 mask on arriving at Heathrow. There was a long wait at Heathrow immigration because many people did not have their arrival documents in order. Brian's documents were in order and he went through immigration quickly when it was his turn. He was not asked to state the purpose of his visit. He was relieved to finally be in England after reading a story about an American woman who was forced to return home after arriving at Heathrow because the immigration officer did not consider her visit to be essential. Brian took a car service to Lee's house where Lee was waiting for him. Lee continued to wear a PAPR for a few days until Brian's tests came back as negative. They were really happy to see each other after so long and their great friendship was as strong as ever.

Epilogue

What would Lee's and Brian's lives have been like if they had never met? Lee painted a bleak picture of this for Brian. He said that he would have continued escorting and could have wound up abusing drugs and maybe even involved in crime. Brian didn't believe that. Lee was just trying to show how much he appreciated Brian's friendship. Brian knew that Lee was a highly intelligent and resourceful person. It might have taken him a little longer to get established without Brian's financial help, but Brian was confident that Lee would have been okay. Without Lee, Brian would have continued to see escorts and might have found no one better than Vladimir, who made it clear to Brian that he was not his friend. As he grew older, he would have become increasingly lonely and depressed. He would not have had much support during his brush with prostate cancer. His isolation during the pandemic, if he had lived that long, would have been intolerable. Yes, Lee and Brian might have survived without each other, but both of their lives were significantly improved by their great friendship.

How can we know that this friendship is genuine? Maybe all that Brian wanted was continuing sexual gratification with a beautiful young man 50 years his junior. Maybe all that Lee wanted was money to buy a house and begin a business as a property developer. They both believe strongly that their friendship is genuine, but that might not be enough to satisfy the most skeptical observer. The real test is whether their friendship would change if their most primitive needs disappeared. As Lee grew richer and Brian grew older, their friendship could no longer be attributed to the needs that first brought them together. Their friendship was never based on just those needs, even from the beginning. It is only to address skeptics that we point out that their friendship was in no way reduced when it was not driven by their primitive needs. Indeed, as Lee became successful in his property development efforts and Brian's physical needs were greatly reduced by the effects of age, their friendship only grew stronger.

Dear reader,

Thank you for reading our true story. We hope that you enjoyed it. It will help us gain a wider readership if you would be kind enough to leave a review on Amazon.

Thanks and best wishes,
Brian and Lee
info@alexanderbrilee.com

Printed in Great Britain
by Amazon